Academic
VOCABULARY
Toolkit

Mastering High-Use Words for Academic Achievement

Dr. Kate Kinsella

with Theresa Hancock

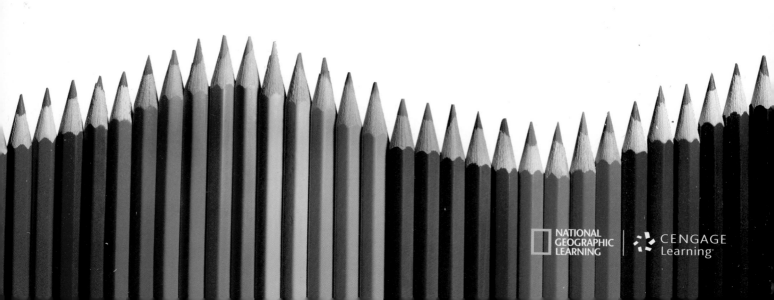

NATIONAL GEOGRAPHIC LEARNING | CENGAGE Learning

Acknowledgments
Grateful acknowledgment is given to the authors, artists, photographers, museums, publishers, and agents for permission to reprint copyrighted material. Every effort has been made to secure the appropriate permission. If any omissions have been made or if corrections are required, please contact the publisher.

Text Credits:
22 "Giant Panda" from *National Geographic Society* online.

Photographic Credits:
Front and Back Cover: ©Victoria Ivanova/ 500px Prime.

Acknowledgments and credits continue on page 180.

For product information and technology assistance, contact us at
Customer & Sales Support, 888-915-3276

For permission to use material from this text or product, submit all requests online at **www.cengage.com/permissions**
Further permissions questions can be emailed to
permissionrequest@cengage.com

National Geographic Learning | Cengage Learning
1 Lower Ragsdale Drive
Building 1, Suite 200
Monterey, CA 93940

Cengage Learning is a leading provider of customized learning solutions with office locations around the globe, including Singapore, the United Kingdom, Australia, Mexico, Brazil, and Japan. Locate your local office at **www.cengage.com/global**.

Cengage Learning products are represented in Canada by Nelson Education, Ltd.

Visit National Geographic Learning online at **NGL.Cengage.com**
Visit our corporate website at **www.cengage.com**

Printed in the USA.
RR Donnelley, Menasha, WI, USA

ISBN: 9781305079335

Printed in the United States of America
16 17 18 19 20 21 22 23
13 12 11 10 9 8 7 6

Contents
at a Glance

Unit 1
Describe

⚑ SMART START

Unit 2
Analyze Informational Text

⚑ SMART START

Unit 3
Cause and Effect

SMARTSTART

Unit 4
Sequence

SMARTSTART

Unit 5
Create

⚑🏁 **SMART** *START*

Unit 6
Compare and Contrast

⚑🏁 **SMART** *START*

Unit 7
Inference

🏁 SMART START

Unit 8
Argument

🏁 SMART START

Describe

To **describe** a person, explain how he or she looks, acts, and what the person says. If possible, include what others think or say about the person.

To **describe** a location or a thing, use your senses to explain how it looks, feels, smells, sounds, and tastes.

 Find It Read the sentences below and underline the words that **describe** a person or a location.

1. Jane is my best friend. She has the longest, darkest, smoothest hair in our class. She talks very fast and laughs at all of my jokes. She is an incredible ballet dancer. Everyone says Jane makes them feel special when she's around.

2. My running shoes are my favorite. The tops have lightweight, black cloth with a bright green symbol. The soles are also green and have rough edges from running on concrete. I love the soft sound they make on the sidewalk when I run to school.

Try It Think about one person you know. Write one important detail in each section of the chart that you would use to **describe** the person.

Says

Others think

Person's Name

Looks

Acts

RATE WORD KNOWLEDGE

Circle the number that shows your knowledge of the words you'll use to describe people, places, and things.

3rd Grade	BEFORE	RATE IT 4th Grade	AFTER	5th Grade
type	1 2 3 4	**character**	1 2 3 4	description
behavior	1 2 3 4	**trait**	1 2 3 4	aspect
physical	1 2 3 4	**appearance**	1 2 3 4	quality
personality	1 2 3 4	**include**	1 2 3 4	characteristic
contain	1 2 3 4	**experience**	1 2 3 4	illustrate
event	1 2 3 4	**location**	1 2 3 4	respond

DISCUSSION GUIDE
- Form groups of four.
- Assign letters to each person. Ⓐ Ⓑ Ⓓ Ⓒ
- Each group member takes a turn leading a discussion.
- Prepare to report about one word.

DISCUSS WORDS

Discuss how well you know the fourth grade words. Then, report to the class how you rated each word.

 Ask

So, _____ what do you know
(NAME)

about the word _____ ?

GROUP MEMBERS **Discuss**

1 = I **don't recognize** the word _____ .

I need to learn what it means.

2 = I **recognize** the word _____ ,

but I need to learn the meaning.

3 = I'm **familiar** with the word _____ .

I think it means _____ .

4 = I **know** the word _____ .

It's a _____ , and it means _____ .
(PART OF SPEECH)

Here is my example sentence: _____ .

 Report Word Knowledge

Our group gave the word _____ a rating of _____ because _____ .

SET A GOAL AND REFLECT

First, set a vocabulary goal for this unit by selecting at least three words that you plan to thoroughly learn. At the end of the unit, return to this page and write a reflection about one word you have mastered.

GOAL

During this unit I plan to thoroughly learn the words _____ ,

_____ , and _____ . Increasing my word knowledge will help

me speak and write effectively when I describe a person, location, or _____ .

As a result of this unit, I feel most confident about the word _____ .

This is my model sentence: _____

_____ .

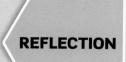 **REFLECTION**

character
noun

 Write it: _____ **Write it again:** _____

 _____

TOOLKIT

Meaning	Examples
the features that make people or things special or different from each other	• When you help someone with a difficult task, it shows your _____ **character**. 
Synonyms • personality; nature	• When you bully another _____, it shows your weak **character**. 

Forms
- **Singular:** character
- **Plural:** characters

Family
- **Noun:** characteristics
- **Adjective:** characteristic

Word Partners
- strong/weak character

- complex character

Examples
- The girl kept playing hard even though she had a sprained ankle. This showed her **strong character**.
- The boy's writing revealed his **complex character**. When I watched him at recess he seemed aggressive, but he wrote very sensitive stories.

 Try It

The gas station attendant showed his strong **character** when he stopped the bully from teasing the

_____.

VERBAL PRACTICE

Talk about it

Discuss
Listen
Write

Discuss ideas with your partner, listen to classmates, and then write your favorite idea.

1. Students who are afraid to speak onstage at an assembly may demonstrate a

_____ character.

2. A good animal shelter volunteer demonstrates (his/her) _____ _____

_____ **character** by showing up on time every Saturday.

WRITING PRACTICE

Collaborate

Discuss
Agree
Write
Listen

Discuss ideas with your partner and agree on the best words to complete the frame. ▶

Some people have complex _____ . For example, a person might

be silly in the classroom but serious on the _____ .

Our Turn

Discuss
Listen
Write

Read the prompt. Work with the teacher to complete the frames. Write a thoughtful response that includes a relevant example. ▶
PROMPT: Leaders often give awards for strong character because of special achievements and community service. What might students do to earn awards for strong character?

Students might be able to earn awards for strong _____ if they do something

that demonstrates a _____ result. For example, a group of

students might speak quietly and act calmly on a field trip in order to promote safety and

_____ on a school bus.

Be an Academic Author

Write
Discuss
Listen

Read the prompt and complete the frames. Strengthen your response with a relevant example.
PROMPT: What are some actions that show a brother's or sister's strong character?

Some actions that show my (brother's/sister's) _____ strong _____

are working hard to get good grades and helping with chores at home. For example, (he/she)

_____ often helps by _____ and

_____ during the week.

Construct a Response

Write
Discuss
Listen

Read the prompt and construct a thoughtful response. Include a relevant example to strengthen your response.
PROMPT: How is your character complex? Explain how you are both brave and kind?

_____

_____

_____

_____

grammar tip ▶

Use the modal verb, or **helping verb**, *might* to show that something is possible. When you use *might*, add a verb in the base form.

EXAMPLE: If it rains on Saturday, we *might* cancel our softball tournament.

trait
noun

 Write it: _____ **Write it again:** _____

 _____

Meaning
a feature or type of behavior

Synonyms
• personality; feature; behavior

Examples
• Being responsible and _____ are two admirable character **traits**.

• Curly _____ and brown eyes are two physical **traits** the twins share.

Forms
• **Singular:** trait
• **Plural:** traits

Word Partners
• character trait(s)

• physical trait(s)

Examples
• Keeping your word and treating others with respect are **character traits** that communities value.
• Gingerbread walls and candy roof tiles are **physical traits** of the house that Hansel and Gretel found in the woods.

 Try It
Planning ahead and being organized are character **traits** of a productive _____ .

VERBAL PRACTICE

Talk about it   Discuss ideas with your partner, listen to classmates, and then write your favorite idea.

Discuss
Listen   1. Being cooperative and _____ are two character
Write
   traits that my partner and I share.

   2. Two physical **traits** that a professional basketball player must possess are

   above-average height and strong _____ .

WRITING PRACTICE

Collaborate

Discuss
Agree
Write
Listen

Discuss ideas with your partner and agree on the best words to complete the frame. ▶

We like to watch movies about people who have strong character _____ .

For example, in the movie _____ , the main character demonstrates

that (he/she) _____ has a/an _____ _____ personality.

Our Turn

Discuss
Listen
Write

Read the prompt. Work with the teacher to complete the frames. Write a thoughtful response that includes a convincing reason.

PROMPT: Think about one character trait that you admire. How would that trait help you?

One character _____ that I admire is being _____ . Having

this trait would help me become better at _____ .

Be an Academic Author

Write
Discuss
Listen

Read the prompt and complete the frames. Strengthen your response with a relevant example. ▶

PROMPT: Think about the traits of an animal you like best. What is one of its important physical traits and its primary character trait?

The animal I like best is (a/an) _____ _____ . One of its important physical

_____ is its _____ . Its primary character

trait is that it is a _____ animal.

Construct a Response

Write
Discuss
Listen

Read the prompt and construct a thoughtful response. Include a convincing reason to strengthen your response. ▶

PROMPT: Think about one cartoon character that you enjoy watching on TV or reading about in the comics. What are his or her physical traits and character traits?

_____

_____

_____

_____

grammar tip ▶

Count nouns name things that can be counted. Count nouns have two forms, singular and plural. To make most count nouns plural, add **-s**.

EXAMPLE: On Saturday, we enjoyed watching the **workers** as they paved the **streets** in my neighborhood.

appearance
noun

Say it: ap • **pear** • ance

 Write it: _____ **Write it again:** _____

 _____

TOOLKIT

Meaning
the way a person
or thing looks

Synonyms
• look

Examples
• You can tell that the girls are
  enjoying the _____
  by their engaged **appearance**.

• To make me laugh, my cousin
  changes his **appearance** by
  stretching the features of his
  _____ .

Forms
• **Singular:** appearance
• **Plural:** appearances

Word Partners
• physical appearance

• describe (my/your/his/her/
  its/our/their) appearance

Examples
• The **physical appearance** of the grocery store was improved after
  the owners installed new signs and lights.
• After my brother returned from a day at the beach, my sister
  described his appearance as sandy and sunburned.

 Try It
The **appearance** of my room was a disaster after my friends _____
_____ .

VERBAL PRACTICE

Talk about it

Discuss Listen Write

Discuss ideas with your partner, listen to classmates, and then write your favorite idea.

1. In many fairy tales and movies, dragons are usually evil characters and have

   _____ physical **appearances**.

2. To attract younger viewers, commercials about new television programs should have a

   character with (a/an) _____ _____

   appearance and details about when to watch the show.

8   Unit 1

WRITING PRACTICE

Collaborate

Discuss
Agree
Write
Listen

Discuss ideas with your partner and agree on the best words to complete the frame. ▶

Five weeks of unusually hot weather changed the _____ of the school's landscape.

The green grass and bushes became _____ and several trees died.

Our Turn

Discuss
Listen
Write

Read the prompt. Work with the teacher to complete the frames. Write a thoughtful response that includes a relevant example. ▶

PROMPT: **When can a character's physical appearance be different from his or her character traits?**

In a book or movie, a character's physical _____ can be different

from (his or her) _____ character traits. For example, in *One Hundred and One Dalmations*,

Cruela De Vil had a beautiful appearance, but her character was actually cruel and

_____ .

Be an Academic Author

Write
Discuss
Listen

Read the prompt and complete the frames. Strengthen your response with a relevant example. ▶

PROMPT: **The setting of a movie demonstrates a certain feeling about the story. If you were a movie director, how would you change the physical appearance of a boring castle so it looks scary?**

If I were a movie director, I would change a boring castle's physical _____

by emphasizing scary details. For example, I would paint the walls _____

_____ , add several frightening

_____ , and break the windows to elaborate that it is unsafe.

Construct a Response

Write
Discuss
Listen

Read the prompt and construct a thoughtful response. Include relevant examples to strengthen your response.

PROMPT: **Without worrying about costs, how would you change the appearance of an old car?**

_____

_____

_____

_____

grammar tip ▶

A **possessive noun** shows ownership. Possessive nouns always have apostrophes. For one owner, add *'s* to a singular noun. For more than one owner, add *s'* to the plural noun.

EXAMPLE: The *bird's* wing was broken so we took it to the animal shelter.

include
verb

 Write it: _____ **Write it again:** _____

 _____

TOOLKIT

Meaning
to make someone or something a part of a larger group or set

Synonyms
• add; combine

Antonyms
• leave out

Examples
• During the party, my friend's mother took a picture that **included** all of the _____ .

• My teacher is happy that the new student's backpack **includes** all the _____ that he needs for school.

Forms
• **Present:**

  I/You/We/They   include

  He/She/It   includes
• **Past:** included

Family
• **Adjective:** inclusive
• **Noun:** inclusion

Word Partners
• include examples (of)

• include information (on/about)

Examples
• For our poster about protecting the environment, our teacher asked us to **include examples of** litter, such as plastic bags.
• The recent broadcast of the Olympics **included information about** how much food each athlete consumes each day.

Try It
A healthy dinner **includes** protein and vegetables, such as broccoli or _____ .

VERBAL PRACTICE

Talk about it   Discuss ideas with your partner, listen to classmates, and then write your favorite idea.

Discuss
Listen
Write

1. The school received a generous art donation that **included** supplies, such as

_____ and blocks of wood.

2. When playing a game online, it is important to **include** players that you know from

your _____ and avoid any strangers.

WRITING PRACTICE

Collaborate

Discuss
Agree
Write
Listen

Discuss ideas with your partner and agree on the best words to complete the frame. ▶

If we were to make a _____ about a superhero, such as

_____ , we would

_____ information about (his/her) _____ ability to

_____ .

Our Turn

Discuss
Listen
Write

Read the prompt. Work with the teacher to complete the frames. Write a thoughtful response that includes a relevant example.

PROMPT: **What should a zoo environment include for its animals?**

Zoos should _____ elements that feel like the natural environment an animal

comes from. For example, a _____ from a tropical rainforest should

have a warm, damp place with lots of _____ .

Be an Academic Author

Write
Discuss
Listen

Read the prompt and complete the frames. Strengthen your response with a relevant example. ▶

PROMPT: **How would you describe a perfect Saturday? Include information on what makes it fun.**

A perfect Saturday would _____ going to a

_____ . For example, when I went to a similar event last year,

everyone was _____ and _____ , including my best friend.

Construct a Response

Write
Discuss
Listen

Read the prompt and construct a thoughtful response. Include a relevant example to strengthen your response. ▶

PROMPT: **Food competitions often require chefs to include odd ingredients to make a new menu item. If you were a chef, what unusual ingredients would you include on a pizza to win the contest?**

_____

_____

_____

_____

grammar tip ▶

Use the modal verb, or helping verb, *would* to show that something is possible. When you use *would*, add a verb in the base form.

EXAMPLE: An ideal vacation *would* be visiting my grandparents and going to a water slide.

experience
noun

Say it: ex • per • i • ence

 Write it: _____   **Write it again:** _____

 _____

TOOLKIT

Meaning something that happens to a person	**Examples** • Riding on the giant _____ was an exhilarating and amazing **experience**.
Synonyms • event; happening	• Having the **experience** of climbing the _____ wall made the boy feel like Spiderman.

Forms
- **Singular:** experience
- **Plural:** experiences

Word Partners
- have (very little, some, a lot of) experience
- previous/prior experience

Examples
- If you **have a lot of experience** taking care of dogs, you know that they require a lot of attention.
- The teacher asked us to help our classmates with their math homework because we had **prior experience** working on fractions.

 Try It

Have you ever had the **experience** of walking into the wrong _____ by mistake?

VERBAL PRACTICE

Talk about it

Discuss
Listen
Write

Discuss ideas with your partner, listen to classmates, and then write your favorite idea.

1. Walking home from school during the storm was (a/an) _____

_____ **experience**.

2. During the assembly, the firefighter described her heroic **experience** rescuing (a/an) _____

_____ from a burning building.

experience
noun

WRITING PRACTICE

Collaborate
Discuss
Agree
Write
Listen

Discuss ideas with your partner and agree on the best words to complete the frame. ▶

One piece of advice we would give to someone with very little _____ playing

_____ is that you need to practice daily to become skilled.

Our Turn
Discuss
Listen
Write

Read the prompt. Work with the teacher to complete the frames. Write a thoughtful response that includes a relevant example. ▶

PROMPT: What prior experiences would a student need to feel confident giving a report to the class?

To feel confident giving a report in front of the class, a student would need several

prior _____ . For example, having opportunities

to write _____ reports and practice presenting them to a

_____ would definitely give the student more confidence.

Be an Academic Author
Write
Discuss
Listen

Read the prompt and complete the frames. Strengthen your response with a personal experience. ▶

PROMPT: Think about the first day of school this year. What made this day a memorable experience?

My first day of school this year was a memorable _____ because it was full of

sights and sounds. When I arrived, I felt both excited and _____ . I saw

teachers greeting students and helping them find their _____ . I also heard

children calling their friends' names and _____ with their classmates.

Construct a Response
Write
Discuss
Listen

Read the prompt and construct a thoughtful response. Include a personal experience to strengthen your response. ▶

PROMPT: What was your most memorable experience this past summer? Describe where you went, what you did, who you were with, and how it made you feel.

_____

_____

_____

_____

grammar tip ▶

Adjectives are always singular even if they describe a plural noun. Do not add **-s** to adjectives that describe plural nouns.

EXAMPLE: Because the teacher had taught science for many years, she always taught *exciting* and *surprising* lessons.

location

noun

Say it: lo • ca • tion

 Write it: _____   **Write it again:** _____

 _____

TOOLKIT

Meaning
the place where something is or where something happens

Synonyms
• place; position

Examples
• My classmate drew a map to show me the right **location** of the _____ .

• After digging several holes, my cousin's dog finally discovered the **location** where he buried his _____ .

Forms
• **Singular:** location
• **Plural:** locations

Family
• **Verb:** locate

Word Partners
• a/the location of

• a/the location where

Examples
• I discovered **the location of** my missing headphones. They were behind my bed.
• When I watch a movie, I prefer to sit in **a location where** no one is talking.

 Try It

Many people use a smartphone to find the **locations** of their favorite _____

_____ .

VERBAL PRACTICE

Talk about it

Discuss
Listen
Write

Discuss ideas with your partner, listen to classmates, and then write your favorite idea.

1. We can use the newspaper to find the **location** where the movie, _____

_____ , is playing.

2. In the mall, you can use the directory at the entrance to find the exact **location** of the

_____ .

WRITING PRACTICE

Collaborate

Discuss
Agree
Write
Listen

Discuss ideas with your partner and agree on the best words to complete the frame. ▶

An online map of my community allows visitors to search for popular _____ ,

such as parks and _____ .

Our Turn

Discuss
Listen
Write

Read the prompt. Work with the teacher to complete the frames. Write a thoughtful response that includes a convincing reason. ▶
PROMPT: Describe the location where you prefer to do your homework.

The _____ where I prefer to do my homework is (my/the) _____

_____ . One reason I like studying in this location

is because I'm not distracted by _____ .

Be an Academic Author

Write
Discuss
Listen

Read the prompt and complete the frames. Strengthen your response with a convincing reason. ▶
PROMPT: Describe an ideal location where you and your friends like to get together.

During our free time, my friends and I enjoy getting together at the _____

_____ . One reason this is an ideal location for us

to spend time together is that we are able to _____

and our parents/guardians don't have to _____ us.

Construct a Response

Write
Discuss
Listen

Read the prompt and construct a thoughtful response. Include examples to strengthen your response. ▶
PROMPT: Write a note to a new student that includes detailed directions so he or she can find the exact location of the principal's office from your classroom.

_____

_____

_____

_____

grammar tip ▶

A **present tense verb** describes an action that is happening now, usually, sometimes, or never. If the subject of a sentence is *he, she,* or *it,* add **-s** or **-es** to the end of a verb.

EXAMPLE: Every summer, my cousin ***plays*** for a softball team and I ***play*** in a marching band.

character

SMART START

character   *noun*

DAY 1

To prepare for the predicted storm, people in my neighborhood showed their

generous _____ by

_____ .

DAY 2

Spending Saturday afternoons at the _____

_____ showed the girl's caring

_____ .

DAY 3

When he denied bullying the new student, he showed that he was cowardly and

_____ . His actions showed that he had a weak

_____ .

DAY 4

Because of his strong, courageous _____ ,

the school honored him with a seat on the stage during the _____

_____ ceremony.

DAY 5

My friend has a complex _____ . When we went to the zoo,

she was bold in the snake house but _____ when

the monkeys screamed while swinging from branch to branch.

TOTAL

◣🏁 SMART START

DAY 1

Laughing at a cruel joke or teasing a _____

shows a weak _____

_____ .

DAY 2

trait   *noun*

The twins had identical physical traits but they had different character

_____ . One was always mischievous while the other was

usually _____ .

DAY 3

The car I hope to own someday would have exciting physical _____

_____ , such as a powerful engine and _____

_____ .

DAY 4

Leopards have several physical _____ . They have dark

spots, huge _____ ,

and snarling teeth.

DAY 5

Different professions require certain key character _____ .

For example, to be a doctor you must be _____ , and to be a

firefighter you need to be daring and dependable.

TOTAL

17

appearance

REVIEW: trait *noun*

DAY 1

The character _____ I look for in a friend are

loyalty and _____

_____ .

appearance *noun*

DAY 2

You could tell that she was tired by her _____

and disheveled _____

_____ .

DAY 3

His _____ showed that he was allergic to

_____

because his face was puffy and his eyes were red and watery.

DAY 4

It is difficult to maintain a tidy and clean _____

when you go on a long, _____

hike or walk.

DAY 5

I didn't recognize my friend at first because her new _____

_____ gave her a completely different

_____ .

TOTAL

⚑ SMART START

DAY 1

REVIEW: appearance   *noun*

Everyone tells me that my physical _____

reminds them of (my/the actor) _____

_____ .

☐

☐

DAY 2

include   *verb*

When you make tacos, it is important to _____ lots

of _____ to

make it extra delicious!

☐

☐

DAY 3

My friend's Halloween costume every year usually _____

some kind of hat to make him look _____

_____ .

☐

☐

DAY 4

Many PG-13 movies _____ language that is not

_____

for elementary school students.

☐

☐

DAY 5

Our teacher said, "If you want to go to the _____ ,

make sure that I _____ your name on the list and

I have a signed permission slip."

☐

☐

TOTAL

experience

SMARTSTART

REVIEW: include *verb*

DAY 1

If we _____ at least seven people in our group, we can use a

coupon to get one person into the new _____

_____ free.

☐

☐

---

experience *noun*

DAY 2

I love to listen to the colorful and engaging stories my _____ tell

about their exciting _____

when they were children.

☐

☐

DAY 3

During the Fourth of July celebration, most people enjoy the _____

of eating _____ and drinking icy

sodas.

☐

☐

DAY 4

Due to his first unforgettable _____ trying to ride

(a/an) _____

and having a bad crash, my neighbor refuses to ever ride one again.

☐

☐

DAY 5

The children in Chicago said that the best _____

of last year was the day schools were closed and they built a snow fort in the

_____ .

☐

☐

TOTAL

**SMART**START

location

DAY 1

REVIEW: **experience** *noun*

The ad said that to apply for the position of _____

_____ you should have two years of _____

and enjoy working with dogs and people.

☐

☐

DAY 2

location *noun*

The _____ of our classroom is (close to/far from)

_____ the _____

_____ .

☐

☐

DAY 3

Some cars are equipped with GPS devices that tell you your _____

and give you directions on how to easily get to places, such as the

_____ .

☐

☐

DAY 4

When you send invitations for special occasions, such as _____

_____ , it is essential to include the

_____ where the event will take place.

☐

☐

DAY 5

If I were the director of an action-adventure movie for children, I would choose a

_____ like _____

because it is always sunny there.

☐

☐

TOTAL

Analyze Informational Text

Analyze means to carefully study.

Informational text can be found in many places, such as articles in a newspaper, magazine, textbook, or even on the Internet. **Informational text** provides important information about something and includes facts.

To **analyze informational text**, be sure to:
- read the title and headings
- read each section, paragraph, or list many times
- carefully study any pictures and charts
- discuss key ideas and important details
- think about what you've learned

 Find It   Read the sample text below. Put a star next to the **informational text**.

 ### Ghost Bear
By Zhou Wei

Mei Lin was half-way up the steep path that led to the peak, when she heard a loud, sudden snap that made her freeze. Could it be a hunter? A farmer? A fellow hiker? Then she heard it again—the sharp snap of a bamboo cane breaking. Mei Lin turned her head slowly to follow the sound and squinted into the dark shadows of the bamboo forest. A flash of white caught her eye. Could this be a real wild panda? Grandfather had seen one when he was a boy, but the villagers all said they were all gone.

PANDAS
By Danielle Berlin

THE GIANT PANDA HAS A HUGE APPETITE FOR BAMBOO. A typical animal eats for 12 hours out of every 24 hour day. It takes 28 pounds (12.5 kilograms) of bamboo to satisfy a giant panda's daily dietary needs. Pandas will sometimes eat birds or rodents as well. Wild pandas live only in remote, mountainous regions of central China, in bamboo forests that are cool and wet. They may climb as high as 13,000 feet (3,962 meters) to feed on higher slopes in the summer season. Pandas are often seen eating in a relaxed sitting posture, with their hind legs stretched out before them. They may appear sedentary, but they are skilled tree-climbers and efficient swimmers.

 Try It   **Analyze** the **informational text** by reading it several times. Then underline important details, and discuss what you learn using the sentence frames.

One important fact that I learned about giant pandas is that they _____ .

Another interesting fact that I learned from this informational text is that they _____ .

RATE WORD KNOWLEDGE

Circle the number that shows your knowledge of the words you'll use to analyze text.

3rd Grade	BEFORE	4th Grade	AFTER	5th Grade
important	1 2 3 4	**focus**	1 2 3 4	significant
topic	1 2 3 4	**essential**	1 2 3 4	section
detail	1 2 3 4	**emphasize**	1 2 3 4	discuss
information	1 2 3 4	**precise**	1 2 3 4	context
fact	1 2 3 4	**message**	1 2 3 4	excerpt
example	1 2 3 4	**major**	1 2 3 4	concept

RATE IT

DISCUSSION GUIDE

- Form groups of four.
- Assign letters to each person.
- Each group member takes a turn leading a discussion.
- Prepare to report about one word.

DISCUSS WORDS

Discuss how well you know the fourth grade words. Then, report to the class how you rated each word.

GROUP LEADER **Ask**

So, _____ what do you know
(NAME)

about the word _____ ?

GROUP MEMBERS **Discuss**

1 = I **don't recognize** the word _____ .

I need to learn what it means.

2 = I **recognize** the word _____ ,

but I need to learn the meaning.

3 = I'm **familiar** with the word _____ .

I think it means _____ .

4 = I **know** the word _____ .

It's a _____ , and it means _____ .
(PART OF SPEECH)

Here is my example sentence: _____ .

REPORTER **Report Word Knowledge**

Our group gave the word _____ a rating of _____ because _____ .

SET A GOAL AND REFLECT

First, set a vocabulary goal for this unit by selecting at least three words that you plan to thoroughly learn. At the end of the unit, return to this page and write a reflection about one word you have mastered.

GOAL

During this unit I plan to thoroughly learn the words _____ ,

_____ , and _____ . Increasing my word knowledge will help

me speak and write effectively when I analyze informational _____ .

As a result of this unit, I feel most confident about the word _____ .

This is my model sentence: _____

_____ .

REFLECTION

focus
noun

Say it: fo • cus

 Write it: _____   **Write it again:** _____

 _____

TOOLKIT

Meaning something or someone that gets the most attention	**Examples** • The new baby was the **focus** of everyone's _____ .
Synonyms • key point; main topic	• The main **focus** of the math lesson was _____ .

Forms
- **Singular:** focus
- **Plural:** foci

Family
- **Verb:** focus

Word Partners
- the focus of

- the main focus of

Examples
- During the soccer game, my friend's comment changed **the focus of** our discussion from the winning goal to who was the best player.
- The life cycle of a plant was **the main focus of** the science lesson.

 Try It

On Thursday night, the **focus** of my attention was on Friday's _____ .

VERBAL PRACTICE

Talk about it   Discuss ideas with your partner, listen to classmates, and then write your favorite idea.

Discuss
Listen
Write

1. When we prepare for a class party, the main **focus** of our plan is making sure we have

    enough _____ that everyone will enjoy.

2. When Harry Potter moved from his room under the stairs and went to school at

    Hogwarts, the **focus** of the story changed from his miserable childhood to his

    _____ adventures learning to be a wizard.

WRITING PRACTICE

Collaborate

Discuss
Agree
Write
Listen

Discuss ideas with your partner and agree on the best words to complete the frame. ▶

The main _____ of many computer games, such as

_____, is to earn enough points to move up to the

next level.

Our Turn

Discuss
Listen
Write

Read the prompt. Work with the teacher to complete the frames. Write a thoughtful response that includes a convincing reason.

PROMPT: Many hit songs focus on the topic of love. What makes this topic so popular?

Romantic love is the _____ of hit songs for many

reasons. For example, the song "_____" is popular

because the topic of love is _____ to most people.

Be an Academic Author

Write
Discuss
Listen

Read the prompt and complete the frames. Strengthen your response with a relevant example. ▶

PROMPT: What event might change the focus of your attention before a test?

If (a/an) _____ _____ happened

right before a test, it would definitely change the _____ of

my attention because I would suddenly feel _____.

For example, my focus would be on the interruption instead of on preparing for the test, and I

would find it difficult to _____ how to answer the questions.

Construct a Response

Write
Discuss
Listen

Read the prompt and construct a thoughtful response. Include a relevant example to strengthen your response. ▶

PROMPT: When you start a science project, what is the main focus of your attention?

_____

_____

_____

_____

grammar tip ▶

The **preposition** *to* needs to be followed by a verb written in the base form.

EXAMPLE: It is important *to* read the directions carefully before you answer the questions on a test.

essential
adjective

Say it: es • **sen** • tial

 Write it: _____ **Write it again:** _____

 _____

TOOLKIT

Meaning	**Examples**
necessary or very important	• It is **essential** that teachers make sure every _____ understands the lesson.

Synonyms
• main; important

Antonyms
• unimportant

• The two most **essential** parts of friendship are to be _____ and loyal.

Family
• **Adverb:** essentially

Word Partners

• most essential _____

• an essential detail

Examples

• One of the **most essential** skills that a painter must have is blending colors.

• Remembering to pack your lunch is **an essential detail** when getting ready for school.

 Try It

Two **essential** ways to become a great _____ player are to go to practice and work hard every day.

VERBAL PRACTICE

Talk about it

    Discuss
    Listen
    Write

Discuss ideas with your partner, listen to classmates, and then write your favorite idea.

1. The most **essential** detail to include on a note explaining a recent absence is that you were

   away from school due to (a/an) _____ _____ .

2. The most **essential** part of our Spanish teacher's lesson was how to ask for

   _____ when traveling in Mexico.

WRITING PRACTICE

Collaborate

Discuss
Agree
Write
Listen

Discuss ideas with your partner and agree on the best words to complete the frame. ▶

The most _____ items to pack for a long, boring car trip are

_____ and plenty of music.

Our Turn

Discuss
Listen
Write

Read the prompt. Work with the teacher to complete the frames. Write a thoughtful response that includes a personal experience. ▶

PROMPT: What is the most essential task when making a dessert for a class party?

When making a dessert such as _____ for a class party,

the most _____ task is to follow the recipe exactly.

Once, I added a cup of salt instead of a cup of sugar, and my classmates

thought my dessert tasted _____ .

Be an Academic Author

Write
Discuss
Listen

Read the prompt and complete the frames. Strengthen your response with a convincing reason. ▶

PROMPT: What is an essential way you have learned about how to make friends at new school?

An _____ way to make friends at a new school is to treat

everyone _____ . One reason is that most kids will feel

_____ when they see that you are friendly, and

they will want to get to know you.

Construct a Response

Write
Discuss
Listen

Read the prompt and construct a thoughtful response. Include a personal experience to strengthen your response. ▶

PROMPT: What do you think is the most essential skill to gain from participating in a sport?

_____

_____

_____

_____

_____

grammar tip ▶

Adjectives are always singular even if they describe a plural noun. Do not add -s to adjectives that describe plural nouns.

EXAMPLE: Cooperation and politeness are two *useful* skills in group work.

emphasize
verb

Say it: em • pha • size

 Write it: _____ **Write it again:** _____

 _____

TOOLKIT

Meaning

to give something special importance

Synonyms
- stress; highlight

Antonyms
- ignore

Examples
- The coaches **emphasized** the importance of _____ your muscles each day.

- The school's newsletter **emphasizes** the importance of recycling _____ bottles.

Forms
- **Present:**
  I/You/We/They   emphasize
  He/She/It   emphasizes
- **Past:** emphasized

Word Partners
- emphasize (my/your/his/her/their) idea/point
- emphasize the importance (of)

Examples
- During the school assembly, the doctor used the phrase "most importantly" to **emphasize her point** about getting a flu shot.
- Before we were allowed to get on the rollercoaster, the attendant **emphasized the importance of** carefully buckling the safety harness.

 Try It

After forgetting to do my homework three times, my teacher **emphasized** the importance of writing each assignment in my _____ .

VERBAL PRACTICE

Talk about it

Discuss
Listen
Write

Discuss ideas with your partner, listen to classmates, and then write your favorite idea.

1. My P.E. teacher tried to **emphasize** the importance of getting to the field quickly by making every student who arrived late run extra _____ .

2. In the morning, many parents **emphasize** the importance of _____

_____ before leaving for school.

emphasize
verb

Collaborate

Discuss
Agree
Write
Listen

Discuss ideas with your partner and agree on the best words to complete the frame. ▶

During recess, the yard duty supervisor always _____ fairness during

a _____ game by making sure each student gets a turn to play.

Our Turn

Discuss
Listen
Write

Read the prompt. Work with the teacher to complete the frames. Write a thoughtful response that includes a relevant example.

PROMPT: **When you share a book report with your class, what is one way you could emphasize what you thought of the book?**

When you share a book report with your class, one way you could _____

your opinion is by reading a paragraph aloud. For example, you could read the most

_____ part of the book to show that the story was

_____ .

Be an Academic Author

Write
Discuss
Listen

Read the prompt and complete the frames. Strengthen your response with a relevant example. ▶

PROMPT: **What are some ways you could emphasize the hazards of pollution for your class?**

One way I could _____ the hazards of pollution for my class would

be to develop a video, or create a _____ . For example,

I could make a video that demonstrates how harmful _____

_____ are to our environment.

Construct a Response

Write
Discuss
Listen

Read the prompt and construct a thoughtful response. Include a relevant example to strengthen your response. ▶

PROMPT: **In a movie or play, what are some ways actors emphasize their feelings without using words?**

_____

_____

_____

_____

grammar tip ▶

A *present tense verb* describes an action that is happening now, usually, sometimes, or never. If the subject of a sentence is *he, she,* or *it,* add *-s* or *-es* to the end of a verb.

EXAMPLE: The speaker *explains* how an elephant *communicates* with people.

precise
adjective

 Write it: _____ **Write it again:** _____

 _____

Meaning	Examples
correct and exact	• The scientist makes very **precise** measurements to complete her _____ .

Synonyms	
• correct	• My uncle used the **precise** directions on the GPS to find the _____ .
Antonyms	
• imprecise	

Family
- **Adverb:** precisely

Word Partners
- give precise details/ information (about)
- precise number of

Examples
- When you share a recipe for cookies, it is important to **give precise details** about how to bake them.
- Our coach told us the **precise number of** exercises we should complete before practice.

 Try It

The scout leader gave us **precise** information about what to bring for our _____ trip.

VERBAL PRACTICE

Talk about it

Discuss
Listen
Write

Discuss ideas with your partner, listen to classmates, and then write your favorite idea.

1. To prepare for the _____ , our teacher gave **precise** details about how to display our project.

2. Since anyone is allowed to join the _____ , it will be difficult to report the **precise** number of athletes.

WRITING PRACTICE

Collaborate

Discuss
Agree
Write
Listen

Discuss ideas with your partner and agree on the best words to complete the frame. ▶

Before we start on a research report, the librarian gives us _____

information about how to locate relevant _____ .

Our Turn

Discuss
Listen
Write

Read the prompt. Work with the teacher to complete the frames. Write a thoughtful response that includes a relevant example. ▶

PROMPT: **How could you determine the precise number of math books in your classroom?**

I could determine the _____ number of math books by totaling

the number of books from different locations in the classroom. For example, by

_____ the number of books in desks and unused books

on the _____ , I would conclude that we have

_____ math books.

Be an Academic Author

Write
Discuss
Listen

Read the prompt and complete the frames. Strengthen your response with a personal experience. ▶

PROMPT: **For safety, what precise information about yourself should you share with your school?**

For my safety, I should share _____ information about where I

live and how to _____ my guardians/parents in an emergency.

Once, when I was in _____ grade, the school

secretary called my house because I had a _____ .

Construct a Response

Write
Discuss
Listen

Read the prompt and construct a thoughtful response. Include a relevant example to strengthen your response. ▶

PROMPT: **When you stay overnight at a friend's house, do you prefer having a precise plan, or do you prefer deciding what to do after you arrive?**

_____

_____

_____

grammar tip ▶

An **adjective** describes, or tells about, a noun. Usually an adjective goes before the noun it describes.

EXAMPLE: If you want people to get to your party, it is important to give *clear* details in your invitation, such as the *exact* number of the house where the party will be held.

message
noun

 Write it: _____ **Write it again:** _____

 _____

TOOLKIT

Meaning
the main or most important idea that someone is trying to tell someone; the theme

Synonyms
- main idea; theme

Examples
- The main **message** on the cover of the magazine is that pollution harms plants and _____ .

- A photographer took this picture to communicate the **message** that helpful friends can make life more _____ .

Forms
- **Singular:** message
- **Plural:** messages

Word Partners
- the central message

- the (writer's/author's) message

Examples
- The **central message** of *Charlotte's Web* is that friendship and love can bring joy to your life.
- In the article about chimpanzees I think **the author's message** is that these animals are in danger of extinction.

 Try It

The main **messages** of my book report are that I learned surprising facts about _____ _____ and that I would recommend it to a friend.

VERBAL PRACTICE

Talk about it

Discuss
Listen
Write

Discuss ideas with your partner, listen to classmates, and then write your favorite idea.

1. The video about playing football had an important **message** about how to use the proper equipment to protect your _____ as you play.

2. One of the main **messages** in the lesson about making friends at school is that you should treat everyone kindly by _____ _____ .

WRITING PRACTICE

Collaborate

Discuss
Agree
Write
Listen

Discuss ideas with your partner and agree on the best words to complete the frame. ▶

In the movie *Brave* the writer's _____ is that it is important for

parents and children to _____ with each other.

Our Turn

Discuss
Listen
Write

Read the prompt. Work with the teacher to complete the frames. Write a thoughtful response that includes a relevant example. ▶

PROMPT: **What could your main message be in an article about responsibility?**

Your main _____ in an article about responsibility could be that

being responsible is gratifying and not _____ . For example, you

could help an older person across a street or you could _____

_____ .

Be an Academic Author

Write
Discuss
Listen

Read the prompt and complete the frames. Strengthen your response with a convincing reason. ▶

PROMPT: **Think about one rule in your classroom that you like. What main message does the rule express?**

I like the rule "Always _____

_____ ." The main message of this rule is to be

_____ . This rule is helpful because it

_____ .

Construct a Response

Write
Discuss
Listen

Read the prompt and construct a thoughtful response. Include a personal experience to strengthen your response. ▶

PROMPT: **Think about a book you read recently. What was the main message of the book? What did the book help you think about or understand?**

_____

_____

_____

_____

grammar tip ▶

Count nouns name things that can be counted. Count nouns have two forms, singular and plural. To make most count nouns plural, add **-s**.

EXAMPLE: While the author included many *ideas* in her book, the most important one was to reuse, recycle, and reduce the use of paper and plastic.

major

adjective

Say it: ma • jor

 Write it: _____   **Write it again:** _____

 _____

Meaning very important	**Examples** • The vet's **major** recommendation is to feed my dog less _____ 
Synonyms • important; serious **Antonyms** • unimportant; minor	• The **major** focus of this photograph is the _____ . 

Family
• majority

Word Partners
• a/the major point

• a/the major reason

Examples
• **A major point** of the lesson was the fact that bees collect nectar from flowers to make honey.
• **The major reason** that the scientist traveled to Brazil was to photograph butterflies in the rain forest.

 Try It

The **major** point of one story I read was that a pet can make a big difference in the life of a _____ person.

VERBAL PRACTICE

Talk about it

Discuss
Listen
Write

Discuss ideas with your partner, listen to classmates, and then write your favorite idea.

1. A **major** point of all our classroom rules is to treat each other and the teacher

_____ .

2. The **major** reason for wearing boots on a rainy day is to keep feet warm and

_____ .

major
adjective

Collaborate

Discuss
Agree
Write
Listen

Discuss ideas with your partner and agree on the best words to complete the frame. ▶

A _____ reason to save your allowance is to

_____ someday.

Our Turn

Discuss
Listen
Write

Read the prompt. Work with the teacher to complete the frames. Write a thoughtful response that includes a convincing reason. ▶

PROMPT: **What major point would you include in a report about a singer, athlete, or author you admire? Why would that be an important point to include?**

One _____ point I would include in a report about

_____ is how much I admire (his/her)

_____ innate ability to _____ . I would also emphasize

that (he/she) _____ is able to _____ very well.

Be an Academic Author

Write
Discuss
Listen

Read the prompt and complete the frames. Strengthen your response with a convincing reason. ▶

PROMPT: **Think about the importance of exercise. What is a major reason to exercise each day?**

A _____ reason to exercise each day is to keep your

_____ strong. This is important because if you don't exercise

regularly you will become _____ .

Construct a Response

Write
Discuss
Listen

Read the prompt and construct a thoughtful response. Include a convincing reason to strengthen your response. ▶

PROMPT: **What major celebration do you enjoy? Why is this celebration important to you?**

_____

_____

_____

_____

grammar tip ▶

Adjectives are always singular even if they describe a plural noun. Do not add *-s* to adjectives that describe plural nouns.

EXAMPLE: Graduation from high school and college are *memorable* events in a student's life.

focus

REVIEW: location   *noun*

DAY 1

When I did not understand why the _____

of the party had changed, my best friend explained why it was moved to the

_____ .

focus   *noun*

DAY 2

After the flood, the _____ of everyone's

attention was on helping people recover from the _____

caused by the rushing water.

DAY 3

Our basketball coach said the two _____ of our

attention should be on teamwork and on _____ .

DAY 4

During lunch, the main _____ of one of our school

rules is not to _____ in the cafeteria.

DAY 5

When I get home from school on Fridays the main _____ of

my attention is to _____ .

TOTAL

 **SMART** START

DAY 1

REVIEW: focus   *noun*

During the reading test, the main _____

of my attention was on the vocabulary section, so I didn't have time to

_____ the comprehension questions.

☐

☐

essential   *adjective*

DAY 2

The whiteboard, books, and _____ are the most

_____ items in my classroom.

☐

☐

DAY 3

Capitalizing the first letter is an _____ detail in

spelling the proper name of a famous person, such as _____

_____ .

☐

☐

DAY 4

To find the most _____ idea in a science article,

it is important to read the title and section headings and

_____ the pictures.

☐

☐

DAY 5

Knowing how to mix ingredients is one _____ skill in

making _____ for a party.

☐

☐

TOTAL

emphasize

DAY 1

REVIEW: essential   *adjective*

When you ask your parents/guardians for money to buy something expensive,

it is _____ to explain your

_____ clearly.

☐

☐

DAY 2

emphasize   *verb*

To _____ the importance of avoiding sugary drinks,

the nurse showed us pictures of children who had serious problems with their

_____ .

☐

☐

DAY 3

Every time I visit my dentist, she _____ the point that

I should _____ my teeth regularly.

☐

☐

DAY 4

I took care of my _____ and cleaned my room to

_____ the fact that I am responsible.

☐

☐

DAY 5

When my dog wants to go for a walk, he _____ the

point by bringing me his _____ .

☐

☐

TOTAL

 **SMART**START

DAY 1

REVIEW: **emphasize**   *verb*

Usually, my teacher _____ the importance of doing

homework every day to practice the _____

skills I learned in class.

☐
☐

DAY 2

precise   *adjective*

The _____ must tell the patient the

_____ number of pills to take each day.

☐
☐

DAY 3

Before we announce the art show, we first need to determine the

_____ number of posters we will need to put up at

school and throughout our _____ .

☐
☐

DAY 4

I used the _____ information I got from my smart

phone to find the new _____ in our town.

☐
☐

DAY 5

My parents arrived at the game at the _____ moment

when our team made the winning _____ .

☐
☐

TOTAL

message

REVIEW: precise   *adjective*

DAY 1

During the canned food drive, our school provided a handout with

_____ details about collection dates and the foods

most needed, such as _____ .

☐

☐

message   *noun*

DAY 2

Winning the soccer match in the rain gave the players a clear

_____ that they can play their best even when the

_____ is not perfect.

☐

☐

DAY 3

Our teacher's main _____ about preparing for the

math test were to _____ all

the lessons and get plenty of sleep.

☐

☐

DAY 4

The main _____ of an assembly about appropriate

computer use could be for all students to avoid _____

_____ .

☐

☐

DAY 5

The dentist's most important _____ to

the patient was to brush after every meal and eat fewer foods that contain a lot of

_____ .

☐

☐

TOTAL

SMART START

DAY 1

REVIEW: message *noun*

In the fable "The Lion and the Mouse," the author described how the mouse

_____ the lion by pulling a thorn out of his paw. The author's

_____ was that even little friends can be great friends.

☐

☐

DAY 2

major *adjective*

Learning about community service and caring for elderly and

_____ people are two

_____ reasons teenagers become volunteers.

☐

☐

DAY 3

The _____ goal of the game Monopoly is to have more

_____ than the other players.

☐

☐

DAY 4

When the weather report predicts a _____ storm, it is

important to have candles, batteries, and _____ .

☐

☐

DAY 5

To earn a _____ part in a school play, you should be able

to remember your lines and _____ well.

☐

☐

TOTAL

Cause and Effect

A **cause** makes something happen.
Ask yourself, "Why did it happen?"
To find the **cause**, look for clue words such as *since*, *because*, and *reason*.

An **effect** is what happens.
Ask yourself, "What happened?"
To find the **effect**, look for clue words such as *so*, *as a result*, and *therefore*.

Find It Read the sentences. Label the cause and the effect.

I forgot to set my alarm clock. ➡ I woke up late for school.

I forgot to set my alarm clock **so** I woke up late for school.
_____ | _____
Cause | Effect

I didn't finish my homework. ➡ I had to stay in at recess.

I had to stay in at recess **because** I didn't finish my homework.
_____ | _____

_____ | _____

Try It Complete the sentences. Then label the cause and the effect in each sentence.

I finished the race first so I won a _____.
_____ | _____

_____ because I saved my allowance.
_____ | _____

RATE WORD KNOWLEDGE

Circle the number that shows your knowledge of the words you'll use to speak and write about cause and effect.

3rd Grade	BEFORE	4th Grade	AFTER	5th Grade
cause	1 2 3 4	**result**	1 2 3 4	impact
effect	1 2 3 4	**affect**	1 2 3 4	factor
problem	1 2 3 4	**consequence**	1 2 3 4	result
solution	1 2 3 4	**lead**	1 2 3 4	alter
happen	1 2 3 4	**occur**	1 2 3 4	influence
change	1 2 3 4	**reaction**	1 2 3 4	outcome

RATE IT

DISCUSSION GUIDE

- Form groups of four.
- Assign letters to each person. Ⓐ Ⓑ
- Each group member takes a turn Ⓓ Ⓒ
  leading a discussion.
- Prepare to report about one word.

DISCUSS WORDS

Discuss how well you know the fourth grade words. Then, report to the class how you rated each word.

GROUP LEADER **Ask**

So, _____ what do you know
(NAME)

about the word _____ ?

GROUP MEMBERS **Discuss**

1 = I **don't recognize** the word _____ .

I need to learn what it means.

2 = I **recognize** the word _____ ,

but I need to learn the meaning.

3 = I'm **familiar** with the word _____ .

I think it means _____ .

4 = I **know** the word _____ .

It's a _____ , and it means _____ .
(PART OF SPEECH)

Here is my example sentence: _____ .

REPORTER **Report Word Knowledge**

Our group gave the word _____ a rating of _____ because _____ .

SET A GOAL AND REFLECT

First, set a vocabulary goal for this unit by selecting at least three words that you plan to thoroughly learn.
At the end of the unit, return to this page and write a reflection about one word you have mastered.

GOAL

During this unit I plan to thoroughly learn the words _____ ,

_____ , and _____ . Increasing my word knowledge will

help me speak and write effectively about Cause and _____ .

As a result of this unit, I feel most confident about the word _____ .

This is my model sentence: _____

_____ .

REFLECTION

result
noun

✏️ **Write it:** _____   **Write it again:** _____

_____

TOOLKIT

Meaning	**Examples**	
something that happens because of something else	• One **result** from staying up late on a school night could be feeling _____ in class.	
Synonyms • effect **Antonyms** • cause	• As a **result** of saving his monthly allowance, my brother was able to buy a _____ .	

Forms
- **Singular:** result
- **Plural:** results

Word Partners
- as a result of (an event)

- _____ . As a result

Examples
- **As a result of** working with a helpful tutor, I'm now getting better math grades.
- I left my backpack at school. **As a result,** I couldn't do my homework.

✏️ **Try It**

As a **result** of extra _____ , the boy played his trumpet perfectly at the concert.

VERBAL PRACTICE

Talk about it   Discuss ideas with your partner, listen to classmates, and then write your favorite idea.

Discuss
Listen
Write

1. We accidentally added _____

_____ to the cake batter. As a **result,** the cake tasted horrible.

2. Our math teacher allowed us to _____

_____ . As a **result,** we all got

good grades on the test.

WRITING PRACTICE

Collaborate

Discuss
Agree
Write
Listen

Discuss ideas with your partner and agree on the best words to complete the frame. ▶

As a _____ of getting a good grade on our science

_____ , our teacher could give each of us (a/an)

_____ .

Our Turn

Discuss
Listen
Write

Read the prompt. Work with the teacher to complete the frames. Write a thoughtful response that includes a personal experience. ▶

PROMPT: **What are some positive results of being helpful at home?**

Two positive _____ of being helpful at home could be feeling appreciated

and being _____ . For example, when I _____

_____

without being asked, my mother says thank you.

Be an Academic Author

Write
Discuss
Listen

Read the prompt and complete the frames. Strengthen your response with a convincing reason. ▶

PROMPT: **What is one negative result from eating too much junk food?**

As a _____ of eating too much junk food, some people experience health

problems. One reason is that foods such as _____ contain a lot

of _____ , which could lead to weight gain.

Construct a Response

Write
Discuss
Listen

Read the prompt and construct a thoughtful response. Include a personal experience to strengthen your response.

PROMPT: **Think about something that you did that made your family proud. Explain the result.**

_____

_____

_____

_____

grammar tip ▶

Use the modal verb, or **helping verb**, *could* to show that something might be possible. When you use *could*, add a verb in the base form.

EXAMPLE: Too much rainfall *could* cause the river to flood.

consequence
noun

Say it: con • se • quence

 Write it: _____ ***Write it again:*** _____

 _____

TOOLKIT

Meaning
something that happens as a direct result of an action

Synonyms
• result, effect

Examples
• One **consequence** of daily exercise might be _____ muscles.

• As a direct **consequence** of the storm, the house was _____ .

Forms
• **Singular:** consequence
• **Plural:** consequences

Family
• **Adverb:** consequently

Word Partners
• a/the consequence(s) (of)

• direct consequence(s) (of)

Examples
• Her first prize award was **a consequence of** her many hours of practice.
• As a **direct consequence of** his nutritious lunch, the boy had plenty of energy all afternoon.

 Try It
Our group cooperated as we worked on our assignment. As a **consequence**, we finished our _____ project on time.

VERBAL PRACTICE

Talk about it

Discuss
Listen
Write

Discuss ideas with your partner, listen to classmates, and then write your favorite idea.

1. A direct **consequence** of the earthquake last week was damaged _____

_____ all over town.

2. If skateboarders don't wear _____ , they may

suffer the **consequences** of pain and a serious injury.

consequence

noun

WRITING PRACTICE

Collaborate

Discuss
Agree
Write
Listen

Discuss ideas with your partner and agree on the best words to complete the frame. ▶

In our experience, if you fail to do your class work and homework on time, you can

suffer negative _____ , such as bad grades and

_____ parents.

Our Turn

Discuss
Listen
Write

Read the prompt. Work with the teacher to complete the frames. Write a thoughtful response that includes a convincing reason. ▶

PROMPT: What could be one consequence of spending a lot of time playing video games?

Learning about characters could be one _____ of

spending a lot of time playing video games. Understanding how characters in games

handle _____ situations can help you write more

_____ stories.

Be an Academic Author

Write
Discuss
Listen

Read the prompt and complete the frames. Strengthen your response with a convincing reason. ▶

PROMPT: Most teachers don't allow students to eat snacks in the classroom. What might be two direct consequences of eating candy and chips in the classroom?

Two direct _____ of eating snacks in the classroom might be

dirty _____ and ants in the classroom. It's hard to focus on the

_____ when the classroom is unsanitary and disgusting.

Construct a Response

Write
Discuss
Listen

Read the prompt and construct a thoughtful response. Include a personal experience to strengthen your response. ▶

PROMPT: What might be a direct consequence of having more classroom computers?

_____

_____

_____

_____

grammar tip ▶

Adjectives are always singular even if they describe a plural noun. Do not add *-s* to adjectives that describe plural nouns.

EXAMPLE: My teacher provides ***clear*** examples of ***new*** words we are learning.

affect
verb

✏️ **Write it:** _____ **Write it again:** _____

_____

Meaning	Examples
to cause a change in someone or something	• Cold weather can **affect** how _____ dress.

Synonyms	
• change	• Studying carefully can **affect** your _____ on a test.

TOOLKIT

Forms
- **Present:**

  I/You/We/They   affect

  He/She/It   affects
- **Past:** affected

Word Partners	Examples
• directly affect	• Getting a good night's sleep **directly affects** how I feel the next day.
• affect how	• Making friends in a new class can **affect how** you feel about going to school.

✏️ **Try It**

The teacher's absence yesterday directly **affected** how well some students behaved in _____ _____ class.

VERBAL PRACTICE

Talk about it

Discuss
Listen
Write

Discuss ideas with your partner, listen to classmates, and then write your favorite idea.

1. The extra _____ directly **affected** the soccer team's performance in the final game.

2. The heavy rainfall **affected** how many vegetables, such as _____ _____ , grew in the garden.

WRITING PRACTICE

Collaborate
Discuss
Agree
Write
Listen

Discuss ideas with your partner and agree on the best words to complete the frame. ▶

Very warm or very cold weather can _____ what we do for fun. In the

winter, we like to _____ .

Our Turn
Discuss
Listen
Write

Read the prompt. Work with the teacher to complete the frames. Write a thoughtful response that includes a relevant example.

PROMPT: **Litter is a problem in many places. How does litter affect the environment?**

Litter negatively _____ the environment because it makes the

environment _____ . For example, when there is trash in a river, such

as plastic bags and _____ , fish and birds are at risk.

Be an Academic Author
Write
Discuss
Listen

Read the prompt and complete the frames. Strengthen your response with a personal experience. ▶

PROMPT: **How can a friend's actions directly affect you?**

A friend's _____ actions can directly _____ how I act.

Recently, I saw a friend helping a student finish her _____ ,

so I decided to also help a classmate.

Construct a Response
Write
Discuss
Listen

Read the prompt and construct a thoughtful response. Include a relevant example to strengthen your response. ▶

PROMPT: **Caring for a dog is a big responsibility. In what ways can caring for a dog affect your life?**

_____

_____

_____

_____

---

grammar tip ▶

Use the modal verb, or **helping verb**, *can* to show that something is possible. When you use *can*, add a verb in the base form.

EXAMPLE: Bringing my lunch to school *can* help my family save money.

lead
verb

Say it: lead

 Write it: _____ **Write it again:** _____

 _____

TOOLKIT

Meaning	**Examples**
to result in something or cause something to happen	• Eating too many treats can **lead** to an upset _____ .
Synonyms	• Regular soccer practice usually **leads** to better _____ .
• cause	

Forms
- **Present:**
  I/You/We/They   lead
  He/She/It   leads
- **Past:** led

Word Partners
- can lead to
- usually leads to

Examples
- A long period of rainfall **can lead to** floods.
- Studying before a test **usually leads to** a better grade.

 Try It

Doctors believe that eating more vegetables and less _____ can **lead** to a healthier body.

VERBAL PRACTICE

Talk about it

Discuss
Listen
Write

Discuss ideas with your partner, listen to classmates, and then write your favorite idea.

1. The scientist hopes that her medical research can **lead** to a cure for _____
_____ .

2. Carefully watching an art teacher demonstrate how to _____

usually **leads** to more creative student artwork.

WRITING PRACTICE

Collaborate

Discuss
Agree
Write
Listen

Discuss ideas with your partner and agree on the best words to complete the frame. ▶

Careful planning for a picnic can _____ to a variety of

_____ and more fun for everyone.

Our Turn

Discuss
Listen
Write

Read the prompt. Work with the teacher to complete the frames. Write a thoughtful response that includes a relevant example. ▶

PROMPT: How can admiring someone's special talent lead you to set a goal for yourself?

Admiring someone's special talent can _____ you to set a goal

for yourself. For example, I greatly admire the ability of _____

to _____ , which motivates me to practice more.

Be an Academic Author

Write
Discuss
Listen

Read the prompt and complete the frames. Strengthen your response with a relevant example.

PROMPT: What kinds of actions usually lead to more friendships?

Being _____ to everyone and treating others fairly are two actions

that usually _____ to more friendships. For example, inviting a new

student to _____ with you is one way to make a friend.

Construct a Response

Write
Discuss
Listen

Read the prompt and construct a thoughtful response. Include a relevant example to strengthen your response. ▶

PROMPT: What is one action that can lead to better study skills?

_____

_____

_____

_____

grammar tip ▶

Use the modal verb, or **helping verb**, *can* to show that something <u>is</u> possible. When you use *can*, add a verb in the base form.

EXAMPLE: Eating a large cafeteria lunch *can* make me feel sleepy during afternoon classes.

occur
verb

Say it:** oc • cur

 Write it: _____ **Write it again:** _____

 _____

TOOLKIT

Meaning	**Examples**
to happen; to take place	• The earthquake **occurred** _____ and without any warning. 
Synonyms • happen	• A fever usually **occurs** when you have the _____ . 

Forms
• **Present:** they occur
  it occurs
• **Past:** occurred

Family
• **Noun:** occurrence

Word Partners
• usually occur(s)

• occurred on/at

Examples
• Forest fires **usually occur** in the summer when the trees are very dry.
• The sunrise **occurred at** 7:02 yesterday morning.

 Try It

My birthday **occurred** on a _____ last year.

VERBAL PRACTICE

Talk about it   Discuss ideas with your partner, listen to classmates, and then write your favorite idea.

Discuss
Listen   1. Bicycle accidents usually **occur** because cyclists don't _____
Write
_____ .

2. The school awards ceremony **occurred** at the end of the _____

_____ .

WRITING PRACTICE

Collaborate

Discuss
Agree
Write
Listen

Discuss ideas with your partner and agree on the best words to complete the frame. ▶

The best part of a story usually _____ when (a/an) _____

_____ event happens.

Our Turn

Discuss
Listen
Write

Read the prompt. Work with the teacher to complete the frames. Write a thoughtful response that includes a relevant example. ▶

PROMPT: What usually occurs after blossoms appear on a fruit tree?

After the blossoms appear on a fruit tree, fruits usually begin to grow. This change

_____ in the springtime. For example, after an apple tree blooms,

_____ apples usually appear where the blossoms have been.

Be an Academic Author

Write
Discuss
Listen

Read the prompt and complete the frames. Strengthen your response with a convincing reason. ▶

PROMPT: When do picnics usually occur in the United States?

In the United States, picnics usually _____ during the month of

_____ . One reason is that the weather is often _____

in the summer, which makes people want to be outside.

Construct a Response

Write
Discuss
Listen

Read the prompt and construct a thoughtful response. Include a relevant example to strengthen your response. ▶

PROMPT: When do celebrations usually occur in your classroom?

_____

_____

_____

_____

grammar tip ▶

A ***present tense verb*** describes an action that is happening now, usually, sometimes, or never. To write a verb in the present tense, add *-s* or *-es* if the subject is *he, she,* or *it*.

EXAMPLE: Every morning my father ***makes*** breakfast and ***washes*** the dishes before he ***goes*** to work.

reaction
noun

Say it: re • ac • tion

 Write it: _____   **Write it again:** _____

 _____

TOOLKIT

Meaning
what someone says, feels, or does because of something that happens

Synonyms
- result; response

Examples
- The expressions on the girls' faces show their **reactions** to the _____ movie.

- Mixing the two chemicals caused a _____ **reaction**.

Forms
- **Singular:** reaction
- **Plural:** reactions

Family
- **Verb:** react

Word Partners
- (my, your, her/his, its, our, their) reaction
- have a positive/negative reaction to

Examples
- When we found our lost puppy, **our reaction** was to hug him tightly.

- My brother **had a negative reaction** to the poison oak leaves he touched in the park. A rash appeared on his skin.

Try It
The kindergarten teacher's immediate **reaction** to the fire alarm was to _____
_____ .

VERBAL PRACTICE

Talk about it

Discuss
Listen
Write

Discuss ideas with your partner, listen to classmates, and then write your favorite idea.

1. When our teacher saw our test results, his **reaction** was to _____
_____ .

2. When I take my pet _____ for a walk, other pet walkers usually have a (negative/positive) _____ **reaction**.

reaction

noun

WRITING PRACTICE

Collaborate

Discuss
Agree
Write
Listen

Discuss ideas with your partner and agree on the best words to complete the frame. ▶

The people in the audience had mixed _____ to the play. Some people

_____ but others thought it was _____ .

Our Turn

Discuss
Listen
Write

Read the prompt. Work with the teacher to complete the frames. Write a thoughtful response that includes a convincing reason. ▶

PROMPT: When bad weather damages homes, what is a common reaction in a community?

When bad weather damages homes, a common _____ in a

community is to collect food and _____ for the victims. One reason

is because most people want to help their _____ .

Be an Academic Author

Write
Discuss
Listen

Read the prompt and complete the frames. Strengthen your response with a convincing reason. ▶

PROMPT: Think about an animated movie you have seen. Did you have a positive or negative reaction to the movie?

I had a (positive/negative) _____ _____ to the movie

_____ . One reason is because I thought the character

_____ was _____ .

Construct a Response

Write
Discuss
Listen

Read the prompt and construct a thoughtful response. Include a convincing reason to strengthen your response. ▶

PROMPT: What would your best friend's reaction be if you won tickets to your favorite singer's or band's concert?

_____

_____

_____

_____

grammar tip ▶

Count nouns name things that can be counted. Count nouns have two forms, singular and plural. To make most count nouns plural, add **-s**.

EXAMPLE: Our neighborhood would feel safer if we had more **streetlights** and **crosswalks**.

result

 **SMART**START

REVIEW: major   *adjective*

DAY 1

One _____ reason I got a good grade on my social

studies report was that I included many _____

that helped explain my ideas.

☐

☐

---

result   *noun*

DAY 2

The only negative _____ of winning the hot

dog eating contest at the fair was that I felt _____

for the rest of the day.

☐

☐

DAY 3

I ate too much _____ and I did not floss my teeth

every day. As a _____ , my dentist found two

cavities at my check up.

☐

☐

DAY 4

To achieve positive _____ on your report card, you

must have appropriate behavior and _____

in every class.

☐

☐

DAY 5

My best friend just finished a training class with his puppy. As a direct

_____ , Rex no longer _____

_____ .

☐

☐

TOTAL

REVIEW: result *noun*

DAY 1

Recently, I spent several hours studying for a _____ .

As a _____ , I earned a good grade.

consequence *noun*

DAY 2

One of the _____

of getting good grades might be receiving _____

from parents or teachers.

DAY 3

Athletes wear safety equipment when they play sports, such as softball and

_____ . As a _____ ,

they have fewer serious injuries.

DAY 4

A sunburn is often a _____

of spending a day at the _____

without wearing sunscreen.

DAY 5

I believe schools should buy more _____

equipment. As a _____ , students might learn how to

_____ .

TOTAL

affect

REVIEW: consequence *noun*

DAY 1

Some schools were closed for three days last _____ as a direct _____ of the huge snowstorm.

☐

☐

affect *verb*

DAY 2

My mother's advice about my report _____ how I revised my _____

_____ .

☐

☐

DAY 3

An assembly about bullying can _____ how _____ treat each other.

☐

☐

DAY 4

Getting plenty of _____ can directly _____ an athlete's ability to compete.

☐

☐

DAY 5

The movie about the tornado showed how an extremely strong wind can

_____ trees and

_____ .

☐

☐

TOTAL

SMART START

REVIEW: affect *verb*

DAY 1

Eating a healthy diet can _____ how you feel and the way

you _____

in school.

lead *verb*

DAY 2

A heavy rain storm can _____ to serious damage to a

school's _____

_____ .

DAY 3

Patience and _____ behavior amongst

athletes can _____

to improved teamwork.

DAY 4

Inviting too many friends over on the weekend often _____

to a lot of _____

_____ .

DAY 5

Young singers who perform on television talent shows hope their performance

_____ to _____

_____ .

TOTAL

occur

REVIEW: lead *verb*

DAY 1

Taking time to organize the _____

for a birthday party usually _____

to a successful event.

occur *verb*

DAY 2

Television commercials about _____

usually _____ right before

summer begins.

DAY 3

In football, winning plays often _____ right after

encouragement from the _____

_____ .

DAY 4

Many action movies contain scenes when danger _____

and _____

need to be rescued.

DAY 5

Before a storm _____ , the sky often turns

_____

and people rush indoors.

TOTAL

SMARTSTART

REVIEW: occur   *verb*

DAY 1

Homework mistakes often _____ when students are not _____ the assignment.

reaction   *noun*

DAY 2

When the batter struck out, the _____ from the crowd showed that they felt _____ _____ .

DAY 3

One _____ my family might have if we won the lottery would be to _____ _____ .

DAY 4

Many students expressed their (positive/negative) _____ _____ to the principal's announcement about the new school mascot by _____ loudly.

DAY 5

When the school changed the date for the _____ , I didn't expect my friends to have such negative _____ _____ .

TOTAL

Toolkit Unit 4 | Sequence

Sequence

Sequence is the order in which events happen. Use the signal words **first**, **next** and **last**, along with the Toolkit Words in this unit to help you analyze, discuss, and write about the **sequence** of events.

🔍 **Find It**   Read the sentences. Determine the sequence and write **1st**, **2nd**, and **3rd** to show the order in which the events happen.

1. _____ My sister found her birthday package.

   _____ So, she checked the mailbox.

   _____ Today is my sister's birthday.

2. _____ Just before dinner, it started to rain.

   _____ So, I took my umbrella to school.

   _____ When we woke up, the sky was dark with clouds.

 Try It   Show the **sequence** by describing something that might occur after the first and second events.

1. First, our family planned a visit to the animal shelter.

2. After we arrived we saw several _____.

3. In the end we decided to adopt a _____.

RATE WORD KNOWLEDGE

Circle the number that shows your knowledge of the words you'll use to speak and write about sequence.

3rd Grade	BEFORE	4th Grade	AFTER	5th Grade
		RATE IT		
order	1 2 3 4	**process**	1 2 3 4	initially
next	1 2 3 4	**final**	1 2 3 4	previously
before	1 2 3 4	**afterward**	1 2 3 4	subsequently
after	1 2 3 4	**following**	1 2 3 4	eventually
finally	1 2 3 4	**previous**	1 2 3 4	ultimately
following	1 2 3 4	**prior**	1 2 3 4	preceding

DISCUSSION GUIDE
- Form groups of four.
- Assign letters to each person.
- Each group member takes a turn leading a discussion.
- Prepare to report about one word.

Ⓐ Ⓑ
Ⓓ Ⓒ

DISCUSS WORDS

Discuss how well you know the fourth grade words. Then, report to the class how you rated each word.

GROUP LEADER **Ask**

So, _____ what do you know
          (NAME)

about the word _____ ?

GROUP MEMBERS **Discuss**

1 = I **don't recognize** the word _____ .

I need to learn what it means.

2 = I **recognize** the word _____ ,

but I need to learn the meaning.

3 = I'm **familiar** with the word _____ .

I think it means _____ .

4 = I **know** the word _____ .

It's a _____ , and it means _____ .
          (PART OF SPEECH)

Here is my example sentence: _____ .

REPORTER **Report Word Knowledge**

Our group gave the word _____ a rating of _____ because _____ .

SET A GOAL AND REFLECT

First, set a vocabulary goal for this unit by selecting at least three words that you plan to thoroughly learn. At the end of the unit, return to this page and write a reflection about one word you have mastered.

GOAL

During this unit I plan to thoroughly learn the words _____ ,

_____ , and _____ . Increasing my word knowledge will

help me speak and write effectively about _____ .

As a result of this unit, I feel most confident about the word _____ .

This is my model sentence: _____

_____ .

REFLECTION

process

noun

 Write it: _____ **Write it again:** _____

 _____

TOOLKIT

Meaning	Examples
a series of actions or changes that happen over time	• The first step in the **process** of cooking something new should be reading the _____ .
Synonyms • plan	• During the field trip, we learned that the **process** for building a _____ is very complex.

Forms
• **Singular:** process
• **Plural:** processes

Family
• **Verb:** process

Word Partners
• the process of
• a process for (doing a task)

Examples
• My science teacher is in **the process of** planning a field trip.
• The **process for** getting a new bus pass is very easy.

 **Try It**

I am in **the process of** getting a new _____ for school because I lost my old one.

VERBAL PRACTICE

Talk about it

Discuss
Listen
Write

Discuss ideas with your partner, listen to classmates, and then write your favorite idea.

1. One important step I always complete in my **process** for getting ready for school is to

_____ before leaving the house.

2. The **process** of learning to tie their own shoes is _____ for

many preschoolers.

WRITING PRACTICE

Collaborate

Discuss
Agree
Write
Listen

Discuss ideas with your partner and agree on the best words to complete the frame. ▶

Our social studies class is in the _____ of learning about

_____ . It's a very

_____ subject!

Our Turn

Discuss
Listen
Write

Read the prompt. Work with the teacher to complete the frames. Write a thoughtful response that includes a personal experience. ▶

PROMPT: What are the first two steps you take in the process of cleaning your room?

I have a simple _____ for cleaning my room. First, I

_____ , then I

_____ .

Be an Academic Author

Write
Discuss
Listen

Read the prompt and complete the frames. Strengthen your response with a convincing reason. ▶

PROMPT: What is one important step you follow in the process of doing your homework?

One important step I follow in the _____ of doing my

homework is _____ . I do

this because it helps me _____ .

Construct a Response

Write
Discuss
Listen

Read the prompt and construct a thoughtful response. Include a personal experience to strengthen your response. ▶

PROMPT: Think about a snack that you like to prepare. Is it a simple or complex process? Describe the steps you take in the process of preparing it.

_____

_____

_____

_____

grammar tip ▶

Use a verb + *ing* after the prepositions *by*, *of*, and *for*.

EXAMPLE: The swimmer got over her fear *of diving by practicing* every day at the pool.

final
adjective

Say it: fi • nal

 Write it: _____   **Write it again:** _____

 _____

TOOLKIT

Meaning
at the end; the last in a series

Examples
- When a foul occurs in a soccer game, the _____ makes the **final** decision about the penalty.

Synonyms
- last; end

Antonyms
- beginning

- The **final** step in baking _____ is taking them out of the oven.

Family
- **Verb:** finalize
- **Noun:** final
- **Adverb:** finally

Word Partners
- final step

- my/your/our/their final ___

Examples
- The **final step** in doing the laundry is putting all the folded clothes away.
- After losing all year, the basketball team won **their final game**.

 Try It
My cousin explained the **final step** in making some _____ for the party.

VERBAL PRACTICE

Talk about it   Discuss ideas with your partner, listen to classmates, and then write your favorite idea.

> Discuss
> Listen
> Write

1. On the **final** day of school, we usually have (a/an) _____ _____ before leaving for summer vacation.

2. The **final** step in my process for getting ready for bed is _____
_____ .

WRITING PRACTICE

Collaborate
Discuss
Agree
Write
Listen

Discuss ideas with your partner and agree on the best words to complete the frame. ▶

Before turning in a _____ report, students should make

sure the _____ is correct.

Our Turn
Discuss
Listen
Write

Read the prompt. Work with the teacher to complete the frames. Write a thoughtful response that includes a convincing reason. ▶

PROMPT: What is one final step you would take to convince your parents to buy you something special for your birthday?

One _____ step I would take to convince my parents to buy me

(a/an) _____ _____ for my birthday would be to remind them that

I have been working hard to _____ . One reason is

my parents believe being _____ is very important.

Be an Academic Author
Write
Discuss
Listen

Read the prompt and complete the frames. Strengthen your response with a relevant example. ▶

PROMPT: What usually happens in the final chapters of a book? What happened in the final chapters of a book you recently read?

The _____ chapters in a book are usually the most _____

part of the story. For example, at the end of the book, _____

_____ , the main character(s)

_____ .

Construct a Response
Write
Discuss
Listen

Read the prompt and construct a thoughtful response. Include a convincing reason to strengthen your response. ▶

PROMPT: Think about an important decision you had to make about summer vacation. What were your choices, and what was your final decision?

_____

_____

_____

grammar tip ▶

An **adjective** describes, or tells about, a noun. Usually an adjective goes before the noun it describes.

EXAMPLE: After thinking it over, I finally decided to keep my *old* bike instead of buying a *new* one.

afterward
adverb

Say it: af • ter • ward

Write it: _____ **Write it again:** _____

_____

TOOLKIT

Meaning	Examples
at a later time; or following something else	• At the festival, people made wishes, and **afterward** they released _____ . 
Synonyms • later; after **Antonyms** • before	• The children worked in pairs to make _____ in their Spanish class. They were able to take some home **afterward**. 

Word Partners
- immediately afterward

- shortly afterward

Examples
- The emergency team lifted the injured skier into the helicopter, and they arrived at the hospital **immediately afterward**.
- My sister graduated from high school when she was eighteen. **Shortly afterward**, she left home for college.

 Try It

On Sunday, my family enjoyed a special meal. **Afterward**, we _____ together.

VERBAL PRACTICE

Talk about it

Discuss
Listen
Write

Discuss ideas with your partner, listen to classmates, and then write your favorite idea.

1. The fire alarm sounded, and **afterward** we all _____ .

2. When I get home from school, I take off my backpack and put it away. Soon **afterward**,

   I _____ .

WRITING PRACTICE

Collaborate

Discuss
Agree
Write
Listen

Discuss ideas with your partner and agree on the best words to complete the frame. ▶

Sometimes, when we work hard to complete our _____

_____ , shortly _____ we need some time to rest.

Our Turn

Discuss
Listen
Write

Read the prompt. Work with the teacher to complete the frames. Write a thoughtful response that includes a personal experience. ▶

PROMPT: **What is the first thing you usually do when you arrive at school on Monday morning? What do you do shortly afterward?**

The first thing I usually do when I arrive to school on Monday morning is _____

_____ . Shortly

_____ , I enter my classroom and prepare for a _____ lesson.

Be an Academic Author

Write
Discuss
Listen

Read the prompt and complete the frames. Strengthen your response with a convincing reason. ▶

PROMPT: **A major storm such as a hurricane or snowstorm can be difficult for a community, during the storm and afterward. If a serious storm damaged your community, what would you expect to happen soon afterward?**

If a serious storm happened in my community, soon _____ I would

expect to see people _____ . I would expect this

because major storms often damage _____ .

Construct a Response

Write
Discuss
Listen

Read the prompt and construct a thoughtful response. Include a personal experience to strengthen your response. ▶

PROMPT: **Think of a holiday that your family celebrates. What is the first thing you do to celebrate? What do you do afterward?**

_____

_____

_____

_____

grammar tip ▶

An **adverb** describes an action and can go before or after a verb. The words *usually, often, shortly,* and *sometimes* are examples of adverbs.

EXAMPLE: My family and I ***usually*** make breakfast together on Saturdays. We ***often*** make pancakes, but we make waffles ***sometimes***, too.

following
adjective

Write it: _____   **Write it again:** _____

_____

TOOLKIT

Meaning	Examples
being next in order or in time; listed or shown next	• The new _____ struck out in the first game, but in the **following** game, he hit a home run.

Synonyms
• next; after

Antonyms
• before

• Our neighbor drove his wife to the _____ late at night, and by the **following** morning, they had a beautiful new baby.

Family
• **Verb:** follow

Word Partners
• the following (day, week, year)
• in the following (item, text, sentence, paragraph)

Examples
• We have a field trip next week and a school picnic **the following week**.
• **In the following sentence**, the subject is underlined: *The crow landed on the fencepost.*

 Try It

The party lasted until midnight. The **following** morning, the living room had _____ everywhere.

VERBAL PRACTICE

Talk about it

Discuss
Listen
Write

Discuss ideas with your partner, listen to classmates, and then write your favorite idea.

1. The **following** three desserts are the ones I prefer the most: _____

   ice cream, _____ pie, and _____ .

2. When I stay up too late on a school night, I'm usually _____

   the **following** day.

WRITING PRACTICE

Collaborate

Discuss
Agree
Write
Listen

Discuss ideas with your partner and agree on the best words to complete the frame. ▶

We love school vacations for the _____ reasons: they give us time to

_____ and _____

with our friends.

Our Turn

Discuss
Listen
Write

Read the prompt. Work with the teacher to complete the frames. Write a thoughtful response that includes a convincing reason. ▶

PROMPT: Think about a place where you enjoy spending time. List the reasons you enjoy spending time there.

On the weekends, I enjoy spending time at _____

for the _____ reasons: First, it is a very exciting place, and second, I can

always _____ there.

Be an Academic Author

Write
Discuss
Listen

Read the prompt and complete the frames. Strengthen your response with a relevant example. ▶

PROMPT: If you had trouble with division this year, what could you do to make sure you improve your skills the following year?

If I had trouble with division in fourth grade, I could make sure I improve the _____

year by _____ all summer. For example, I could

_____ to help me improve my skills.

Construct a Response

Write
Discuss
Listen

Read the prompt and construct a thoughtful response. Include a relevant example to strengthen your response. ▶

PROMPT: When you have an argument with a friend, it can create bad feelings. If you had an argument with a friend, what could you do the following day to make things better?

_____

_____

_____

_____

grammar tip ▶

Adjectives are always singular even if they describe a plural noun. Do not add **-s** to adjectives that describe plural nouns.

EXAMPLE: The *opening* passages from the novel describe the *two main* characters.

previous
adjective

Write it: _____ **Write it again:** _____

_____

TOOLKIT

Meaning

happening before something else

Synonyms

- earlier

Antonyms

- following

Examples

- My little brother went to school with crutches yesterday because of his skateboarding

  _____

  the **previous** day.

- The new _____ are helping the high school students learn more than they did the **previous** year.

Family

- **Adverb:** previously

Word Partners

- previous day/week/ month/year
- previous (event)

Examples

- Our baseball team lost this week, but we won the **previous week.**

- I was nervous about my dentist appointment this morning because at my **previous appointment** I learned I had a cavity.

 Try It

In **previous** years, I enjoyed reading _____ books, but now I prefer _____ books.

VERBAL PRACTICE

Talk about it

Discuss Listen Write

Discuss ideas with your partner, listen to classmates, and then write your favorite idea.

1. In this class, we're studying vocabulary. In my **previous** class, we were studying

   _____ .

2. If you missed the **previous** episode of _____ ,

   I can summarize it for you before you watch this week's show.

WRITING PRACTICE

Collaborate

Discuss
Agree
Write
Listen

Discuss ideas with your partner and agree on the best words to complete the frame. ▶

This year, many students are wearing _____ .

The _____ year, _____ were popular.

Our Turn

Discuss
Listen
Write

Read the prompt. Work with the teacher to complete the frames. Write a thoughtful response that includes a relevant example. ▶

PROMPT: What do you usually do at the beginning of each year to show what you learned the previous year?

At the beginning of the school year, we usually review what we learned the _____

year. For example, at the beginning of this year, we reviewed _____

_____ in our _____ class.

Be an Academic Author

Write
Discuss
Listen

Read the prompt and complete the frames. Strengthen your response with a convincing reason. ▶

PROMPT: Compare your favorite lunch item from the cafeteria menu with a previous selection that you did not enjoy.

My favorite lunch item on the cafeteria menu is _____ .

A _____ selection that I did not enjoy was _____

because it was _____ and _____ .

Construct a Response

Write
Discuss
Listen

Read the prompt and construct a thoughtful response. Include a convincing reason to strengthen your response. ▶

PROMPT: Compare one major assignment from this school year to one from a previous year. Describe the assignment, and what made one more difficult than the other.

_____

_____

_____

_____

grammar tip ▶

An **adjective** describes, or tells about, a noun. Usually an adjective goes before the noun it describes.

EXAMPLE: My *older* brother talked for a *long* time to our *new* neighbor.

prior
adjective

✏️ **Write it:** _____ **Write it again:** _____

🌐 _____

TOOLKIT

Meaning happening earlier	**Examples** • **Prior** to the big football game, a marching _____ played the National Anthem.

Synonyms • previous; past; earlier **Antonyms** • later; following	• When my bike's front _____ became stuck, I used my **prior** knowledge about gears and oil to fix it.

Word Partners
- prior to
- prior knowledge (of/about)

Examples
- **Prior to** the math quiz, we did a few word problems to practice.
- When my father came to the United States, he had no **prior knowledge of** English, but he became fluent within three years.

✏️ **Try It**

Prior to eating dinner, I usually _____.

VERBAL PRACTICE

Talk about it

Discuss
Listen
Write

Discuss ideas with your partner, listen to classmates, and then write your favorite idea.

1. Although I had no **prior** knowledge about the game, I still won the first time

   I played _____ .

2. **Prior** to moving to this city, some of my family members lived in

   _____ .

WRITING PRACTICE

Collaborate

Discuss
Agree
Write
Listen

Discuss ideas with your partner and agree on the best words to complete the frame. ▶

Our new science teacher has _____ knowledge about _____ because

she worked as a research scientist in (a/an) ____ _____ .

Our Turn

Discuss
Listen
Write

Read the prompt. Work with the teacher to complete the frames. Write a thoughtful response that includes a personal experience. ▶

PROMPT: Imagine that you are competing in the school spelling bee next week. What would you do prior to the competition in order to prepare?

One thing I would do _____ to competing in the spelling bee is

_____ . This worked when I had an

important _____ test, because practicing helped me feel more confident.

Be an Academic Author

Write
Discuss
Listen

Read the prompt and complete the frames. Strengthen your response with a relevant example. ▶
PROMPT: Imagine that you lost an important homework assignment. What is one thing you would do prior to getting a bad grade?

If I lost an important homework assignment, one thing I would do _____ to

getting a bad grade would be to ask my teacher for _____ .

For example, once I was absent because I _____

_____ and my teacher was very helpful and understanding.

Construct a Response

Write
Discuss
Listen

Read the prompt and construct a thoughtful response. Include a relevant example to strengthen your response.
PROMPT: Imagine you're planning a party at your house. There are certain activities you need to do to prepare. What are three things you would do prior to the event?

_____

_____

_____

_____

grammar tip ▶

A **past-tense verb** tells about an action that already happened. To write the past tense, add *-ed* at the end of a verb.

EXAMPLE: What *happened* during the big fight on the playground?

process

REVIEW: reaction   *noun*

DAY 1

My immediate _____ upon seeing the adorable puppies in

the pet store was to _____ .

process   *noun*

DAY 2

My family is in the _____ of buying a new

_____ .

DAY 3

My first step in the _____ of studying

_____

is to make flashcards.

DAY 4

The _____ of making

_____ out of paper is very simple.

DAY 5

My sister is in the _____ of getting her license so she can

_____ this summer.

TOTAL

76

🏁 **SMART**START

REVIEW: process   *noun*

DAY 1

Our new art teacher explained the _____ for making colorful

_____ .

☐
☐

final   *adjective*

DAY 2

Everyone waited to hear the _____ decision from the Olympic

judges about who won the _____ event.

☐
☐

DAY 3

On the _____ day before the music competition, the contestants

spent their time _____ .

☐
☐

DAY 4

When my mother is wrapping a gift, her _____

step is to add a _____ to it.

☐
☐

DAY 5

We can't play outside today because the _____ drafts of

our _____

are due tomorrow.

☐
☐

TOTAL

afterward

SMART START

REVIEW: final   *adjective*

DAY 1

At the track meet, my _____

was losing the 100 yard dash, until the _____

moment when she raced ahead and crossed the finish line first.

afterward   *adverb*

DAY 2

If you take _____

lessons this year and practice every day, _____

you will probably be good at it.

DAY 3

If you eat too much _____ , you will

probably feel sick _____ .

DAY 4

At the birthday party, we sang and watched our friend open presents. Shortly

_____ ,

we all _____ .

DAY 5

On a hot day, when I've been _____

and sweating for a while outside, I always drink plenty of water _____ .

TOTAL

 **SMART**START

DAY 1

REVIEW: afterward   *adverb*

I thought it would be fun to watch a _____ movie on TV, but

_____ I couldn't sleep.

☐
☐

DAY 2

following   *adjective*

I received an amazing gift in the mail from _____ .

The _____ day,

I called (him/her/them) _____ to say thank you.

☐
☐

DAY 3

I missed school once because I had _____ .

On the _____

day, I had to work extra hard to catch up.

☐
☐

DAY 4

I'm going to do the _____ two activities this

weekend: relaxing and _____ .

☐
☐

DAY 5

When I was in first grade, I learned how to do addition and subtraction. Then the

_____ year, I learned how to

_____ .

☐
☐

TOTAL

🏁 SMART START

DAY 1

REVIEW: following   *adjective*

The sixth graders were rude to the substitute teacher, so the _____

day the principal made them _____ .

☐
☐

DAY 2

previous   *adjective*

The _____ owners of the house left behind

_____ for the new owners to use.

☐
☐

DAY 3

Right now, everyone wants to go see the movie _____

_____ .

The _____ year, *Frozen* was the movie that everyone wanted to see.

☐
☐

DAY 4

The cartoon that's on TV now is much _____

than the _____ cartoon was.

☐
☐

DAY 5

I couldn't go to the _____ because I was sick the

_____ night.

☐
☐

TOTAL

⚑⚑ SMART START

DAY 1

REVIEW: previous   *adjective*

The new student was sent to the principal's office for _____

_____ ,

but the principal let him go because he had no _____

record of misbehaving.

prior   *adjective*

DAY 2

I used the few minutes in class _____ to the test to

_____ for it.

DAY 3

All students need to get signed permission slips from their parents or guardians

_____ to the field trip to _____ .

DAY 4

We usually get _____ at the concession stand

_____ to going into the theater and watching the movie.

DAY 5

My _____ knowledge of plants and animals helped me to avoid

_____ during our nature hike in the woods.

| TOTAL |
| |

Create

Create means to make something.

To **create** a plan, solution, or an explanation you need to think carefully and consider different ways to answer a question.

To **create** stories, poems, and other pieces of writing you need to use your imagination and explore many ideas.

 Find It   Read the sample tasks below and circle the steps that would help you **create** a strong response.

1. Think about the story Jack and the Beanstalk and write a different ending
   a. review the plot and think of way for Jack and the Giant to become friends
   b. change the name of each character
   c. make up a song about the Giant

2. Explain why exercise is important. Include two details to support your answer.
   a. think of two ways that exercise helps people stay healthy
   b. write about my favorite kinds of exercise
   c. write a sentence about your P.E. teacher

 Try It   **Create** a plan to convince your principal to add ten minutes to the lunch recess.

Reasons Why Students Need a _____ **Recess**

1. long _____ line takes up the entire recess
2. kids need time to _____ with friends
3. young minds need a break from _____
4. teachers need a _____
5. exercise helps students _____ in afternoon classes
6. chance to _____ during recess

RATE WORD KNOWLEDGE

Circle the number that shows your knowledge of the words you'll use as you create plans, solutions, stories, poems, and other pieces of writing.

3rd Grade	BEFORE	4th Grade	AFTER	5th Grade
complete	1 2 3 4	**present**	1 2 3 4	produce
task	1 2 3 4	**develop**	1 2 3 4	propose
prepare	1 2 3 4	**provide**	1 2 3 4	collaborate
provide	1 2 3 4	**revise**	1 2 3 4	accomplish
organize	1 2 3 4	**demonstrate**	1 2 3 4	create
response	1 2 3 4	**elaborate**	1 2 3 4	strategy

RATE IT

DISCUSSION GUIDE
- Form groups of four.
- Assign letters to each person.
- Each group member takes a turn leading a discussion.
- Prepare to report about one word.

Ⓐ Ⓑ
Ⓓ Ⓒ

DISCUSS WORDS

Discuss how well you know the fourth grade words. Then, report to the class how you rated each word.

GROUP LEADER | **Ask**

So, _____ what do you know
(NAME)

about the word _____ ?

GROUP MEMBERS | **Discuss**

1 = I **don't recognize** the word _____ .

I need to learn what it means.

2 = I **recognize** the word _____ ,

but I need to learn the meaning.

3 = I'm **familiar** with the word _____ .

I think it means _____ .

4 = I **know** the word _____ .

It's a _____ , and it means _____ .
(PART OF SPEECH)

Here is my example sentence: _____ .

REPORTER | **Report Word Knowledge**

Our group gave the word _____ a rating of _____ because _____ .

SET A GOAL AND REFLECT

First, set a vocabulary goal for this unit by selecting at least three words that you plan to thoroughly learn.
At the end of the unit, return to this page and write a reflection about one word you have mastered.

GOAL

During this unit I plan to thoroughly learn the words _____ ,

_____ , and _____ . Increasing my word knowledge will

help me speak and write effectively when I create plans and _____ .

As a result of this unit, I feel most confident about the word _____ .

This is my model sentence: _____

_____ .

REFLECTION

present

verb

 Write it: _____   **Write it again:** _____

 _____

Meaning
to talk or write about something; to give or show something

Synonyms
• give; show

Examples
• The coach was proud to **present** the _____ to her team.

• The judge asked the detective to clearly **present** the _____ he found at the crime scene.

Forms
• **Present:**

| I/You/We/They | present |
| He/She/It | presents |

• **Past:** presented

Family
• **Noun:** presenter; presentation

Word Partners
• present (an) idea(s)
• clearly present

Examples
• We will each have a chance to **present an idea** for the class party.
• The newspaper article **clearly presented** information about the extraordinary new robot that the university students had built.

 Try It

On Monday, I have to **present** my speech to the whole class, and I feel _____ .

VERBAL PRACTICE

Talk about it

Discuss
Listen
Write

Discuss ideas with your partner, listen to classmates, and then write your favorite idea.

1. Before we begin our exhibit for the art fair, I will **present** my idea for an exciting

_____ to my group.

2. During the safety drill, the fire chief clearly **presented** information on how to

_____ during an earthquake.

WRITING PRACTICE

Collaborate

Discuss
Agree
Write
Listen

Discuss ideas with your partner and agree on the best words to complete the frame. ▶

In our opinion, an interactive whiteboard is better than a chalkboard because it allows the

teacher to clearly _____ information for the lesson using _____ .

Our Turn

Discuss
Listen
Write

Read the prompt. Work with the teacher to complete the frames. Write a thoughtful response that includes a convincing reason. ▶

PROMPT: **What is one thing you could do to prepare to present a speech?**

One thing I could do to prepare to _____ a speech is to

_____ . The main reason I would do

this is because it helps me to _____ .

Be an Academic Author

Write
Discuss
Listen

Read the prompt and complete the frames. Strengthen your response with a relevant example. ▶

PROMPT: **What can guest speakers do to clearly present information during an assembly?**

Guest speakers can clearly _____ their information

by showing _____ during an assembly. For example,

if someone is giving a presentation about the Solar System, they could present

_____

to help the students follow their ideas.

Construct a Response

Write
Discuss
Listen

Read the prompt and construct a thoughtful response. Include a valid reason to strengthen your response. ▶

PROMPT: **There are many ways of presenting information to make it more fun for the audience. What could you do to make a presentation about your favorite book more fun for your classmates?**

_____

_____

_____

_____

grammar tip ▶

The preposition *to* needs to be followed by a verb written in the base form.

EXAMPLE: Try *to put* your ideas in a logical order. This helps your readers *to follow* them.

develop
verb

Say it: de • vel • op

 Write it: _____   **Write it again:** _____

 _____

TOOLKIT

Meaning

to make something clearer or more complete; to plan a way to do something

Synonyms
- build; make clear

Antonyms
- destroy

Examples
- The gymnastics coach is helping the _____ **develop** routines for the meet.
- The toy inventor **developed** his ideas into a fun _____ helicopter.

Forms
- **Present:**
  I/You/We/They   develop
  He/She/It   develops
- **Past:** developed

Family
- **Noun:** development

Word Partners
- develop an idea (point, topic, sentence)
- develop a plan

Examples
- When you **develop a topic** for a report, you can brainstorm important details to include.
- The group worked together to **develop a plan** for the boat ride.

 Try It

You can **develop** a plan for the weekend by asking your _____ for suggestions.

VERBAL PRACTICE

Talk about it   Discuss ideas with your partner, listen to classmates, and then write your favorite idea.

Discuss
Listen
Write

1. To **develop** their reading skills, students should read a wide variety of materials including

_____ .

2. I'd like to **develop a plan** for becoming (a/an) _____

_____ .

WRITING PRACTICE

Collaborate

Discuss
Agree
Write
Listen

Discuss ideas with your partner and agree on the best words to complete the frame. ▶

To organize a party with your friends, you should _____ a plan that

includes a list of _____ .

Our Turn

Discuss
Listen
Write

Read the prompt. Work with the teacher to complete the frames. Write a thoughtful response that includes a convincing reason. ▶

PROMPT: **What should you do to develop a well-written report?**

To _____ a well-written report, I should start with a clear topic.

Then I need to include _____ to support that topic. For example,

if I want to write a report about one kind of dinosaur, I should include details about its

_____ and _____ .

Be an Academic Author

Write
Discuss
Listen

Read the prompt and complete the frames. Strengthen your response with a relevant example. ▶

PROMPT: **When developing an idea for a science project, what should you think about?**

When I am _____ an idea for a science project, I try to think

about what would be (a/an) _____ _____ and what

_____ I will need. For example, I could use objects I find at home

to make (a/an) _____ _____ .

Construct a Response

Write
Discuss
Listen

Read the prompt and construct a thoughtful response. Include a valid reason to strengthen your response. ▶

PROMPT: **Many adults think some children's activities are a waste of time. Choose a game or activity that you enjoy, and explain how it helps you develop important skills and abilities.**

_____

_____

_____

grammar tip ▶

Count nouns name things that can be counted. Count nouns have two forms, singular and plural. To make most count nouns plural, add **-s**. To make count nouns that end in *x, ch, sh, ss,* and *z,* plural, add **-es**.

EXAMPLE: As I blew out the *candles* on my birthday cake, I made three *wishes* for the coming year.

provide

verb

Say it:* pro • vide

 Write it: _____ **Write it again:** _____

_____

TOOLKIT

Meaning

to give something that someone needs or wants

Synonyms

• give; present

Examples

• At tonight's meeting, the club leader will **provide** details about our _____ trip.

• Each member of the _____ should **provide** ideas for the project.

Forms

• **Present:**

| I/You/We/They | provide |
| He/She/It | provides |

• **Past:** provided

Family

• **Noun:** provider

Word Partners

• provide information (on or about)

• provide _____ with _____

Examples

• Last month, the garbage company **provided information about** how to dispose of old paint.

• We need to **provide** the camp director **with** our home phone number.

 Try It

I can easily **provide** information about _____ because it is my favorite topic.

VERBAL PRACTICE

Talk about it

> Discuss
> Listen
> Write

Discuss ideas with your partner, listen to classmates, and then write your favorite idea.

1. My teacher usually **provides** enough time for us to _____

_____ .

2. When you write a letter to a friend you should **provide** (a/an) _____

_____ on the envelope.

provide
verb

WRITING PRACTICE

Collaborate

Discuss
Agree
Write
Listen

Discuss ideas with your partner and agree on the best words to complete the frame. ▶

We agreed that parents who refuse to let their children _____

should _____ a convincing reason.

Our Turn

Discuss
Listen
Write

Read the prompt. Work with the teacher to complete the frames. Write a thoughtful response that includes a convincing reason. ▶
PROMPT: Why is it important for food companies to provide customers with information about the ingredients in their products?

Companies should _____ information about the ingredients in their products so

people can make better decisions about what to _____ . For example, a

person might want to stay away from certain ingredients, such as _____

because they have (a/an) _____ _____ .

Be an Academic Author

Write
Discuss
Listen

Read the prompt and complete the frames. Strengthen your response with a relevant example.
PROMPT: Imagine you have an assignment to write a report about your town. What are two interesting facts that you will provide about your town?

For my report, I will _____ interesting information about our town. One

interesting fact is that our town has an old historical _____ .

In addition, we also have a new _____

that many people appreciate.

Construct a Response

Write
Discuss
Listen

Read the prompt and construct a thoughtful response. Include a convincing reason to strengthen your response. ▶
PROMPT: When your teachers correct your school work they usually provide information about what you did well and what mistakes you made. Why is it important for teachers to provide students with feedback about their work?

_____

_____

_____

---

grammar tip ▶ Use the **modal verb**, or helping verb, *should* to show that something must happen. When you use *should*, add a verb in the base form.

EXAMPLE: Our town *should do* more to support school athletic programs.

revise
verb

Say it: re • vise

Write it: _____   **Write it again:** _____

_____

TOOLKIT

Meaning	**Examples**
to change something to make it better	• We need to **revise** our plans for the _____ because the bowling alley is already booked.

Synonyms	
• improve; correct	• The _____ are working together to **revise** their science project.

Forms
- **Present:**
  I/You/We/They   revise
  He/She/It   revises
- **Past:** revised

Family
- **Noun:** revision

Word Partners
- have to/need to revise

- revise (my/your/our) _____

Examples
- We **had to revise** the menu for our party when we learned that three of the guests are vegetarians.
- After writing a first draft, I always **revise my paragraph** by checking my spelling and adding interesting details.

✏️ Try It

My cousin and I had to **revise** our plans to see the new movie because we couldn't

_____ .

VERBAL PRACTICE

Talk about it

Discuss
Listen
Write

Discuss ideas with your partner, listen to classmates, and then write your favorite idea.

1. The coach **revised** the game roster because our star _____

   was hurt and couldn't play.

2. My partner recommended that I **revise** my paragraph by adding

   _____ .

revise

verb

WRITING PRACTICE

Collaborate

Discuss
Agree
Write
Listen

Discuss ideas with your partner and agree on the best words to complete the frame. ▶

Unfortunately, teenagers sometimes have to _____ their plans for the weekend

when they _____ .

Our Turn

Discuss
Listen
Write

Read the prompt. Work with the teacher to complete the frames. Write a thoughtful response that includes a convincing reason. ▶

PROMPT: **When might you have to revise your writing more than once?**

Sometimes you need to _____ your writing many times before

it's _____ . For example, I once wrote a third draft I thought was

_____ , but after I got it back from my teacher I saw that it was

full of _____ .

Be an Academic Author

Write
Discuss
Listen

Read the prompt and complete the frames. Strengthen your response with a relevant example. ▶

PROMPT: **Revising your reports is not always easy. What tools can you use to make the job easier?**

When I'm _____ my report, I can check my _____ by reviewing

the lessons in my textbook. I could also ask _____ to read my

paper and give me _____ .

Construct a Response

Write
Discuss
Listen

Read the prompt and construct a thoughtful response. Include a valid reason to strengthen your response. ▶

PROMPT: **What you first think about a person you meet is not always correct. When might you need to revise your thinking about someone?**

_____

_____

_____

_____

grammar tip ▶

The preposition **to** needs to be followed by a verb written in the base form.

EXAMPLE: The child wanted **to make** a card for his father, so he asked his mother **to help** him.

demonstrate
verb

Say it: dem • on • strate

 Write it: _____ **Write it again:** _____

 _____

Meaning	Examples
to show how to do something	• After taking lessons all month, the girl was ready to **demonstrate** her _____ abilities. 
Synonyms • show; explain	• On his TV show, the chef clearly **demonstrated** how to _____ a delicious and healthy pizza.

TOOLKIT

Forms
- **Present:**
  I/You/We/They demonstrate
  He/She/It demonstrates
- **Past:** demonstrated

Family
- **Noun:** demonstration

Word Partners
- demonstrate how to
- demonstrate (my, your, his, her, our, their) ability/ knowledge/skill

Examples
- My math teacher **demonstrated how to** solve the word problem.
- In the talent show, I **demonstrated my ability** to tell jokes.

 Try It

I can **demonstrate** how to _____ because I have a lot of experience.

VERBAL PRACTICE

Talk about it

Discuss
Listen
Write

Discuss ideas with your partner, listen to classmates, and then write your favorite idea.

1. The A+ grade clearly **demonstrated** that I had _____ for the vocabulary test.

2. A mother kangaroo must **demonstrate** how to _____ for her babies.

demonstrate
verb

Collaborate

Discuss
Agree
Write
Listen

Discuss ideas with your partner and agree on the best words to complete the frame. ▶

The best way to learn a difficult skill such as _____ is to ask an

expert to _____ how to do it.

Our Turn

Discuss
Listen
Write

Read the prompt. Work with the teacher to complete the frames. Write a thoughtful response that includes a convincing reason.

PROMPT: **How do you demonstrate that you are a good friend? Why is friendship important to you?**

One way that I _____ that I'm a good friend is by being

_____ . Friendship is important to me because having friends who

_____ helps me feel _____

about myself.

Be an Academic Author

Write
Discuss
Listen

Read the prompt and complete the frames. Strengthen your response with a relevant example. ▶

PROMPT: **How do you demonstrate your abilities in your favorite school subject?**

I _____ my abilities in _____

class by making an effort and doing good work. For example, when I have to write

_____ , I usually work

hard to _____ .

Construct a Response

Write
Discuss
Listen

Read the prompt and construct a thoughtful response. Include a valid reason to strengthen your response. ▶

PROMPT: **Think about a time that you had to perform in front of an audience. Were you in a talent show or contest? How did you demonstrate your skills and abilities?**

_____

_____

_____

_____

grammar tip ▶

A **common noun** names a person, place, thing, or idea. **Singular nouns** name one person, place, thing, or idea. The words *a*, *an*, and *the* often appear before a singular noun.

EXAMPLE: *An* ostrich is *a* large flightless bird native to *the* continent of Africa.

elaborate

verb

Say it: e • lab • o • rate

 Write it: _____ **Write it again:** _____

 _____

TOOLKIT

Meaning	**Examples**
to give more details about or explain	• The _____ used a poster to **elaborate** on her ideas.
Synonyms	• Writers **elaborate** on important ideas to help their _____ understand them.
• explain; develop	

Forms
- **Present:**
  - I/You/We/They elaborate
  - He/She/It elaborates
- **Past:** elaborated

Family
- **Noun:** elaboration

Word Partners
- elaborate on
- need to elaborate (on)

Examples
- The dog trainer **elaborated on** his process to train puppies to sit by demonstrating with a young dalmatian.
- After noticing that my brother did not understand the new microwave, I realized that I **needed to elaborate** on how to set the timer.

 Try It

The gardener **elaborated** on his plans for the school's new planter box by showing us pictures of the _____ he wanted to include.

VERBAL PRACTICE

Talk about it

Discuss ideas with your partner, listen to classmates, and then write your favorite idea.

Discuss
Listen
Write

1. One way to **elaborate** on a description about the main character in a novel is to add

_____ .

2. We were all very confused about the _____ so our teacher

realized that she needed to **elaborate** on her expectations.

WRITING PRACTICE

Collaborate

Discuss
Agree
Write
Listen

Discuss ideas with your partner and agree on the best words to complete the frame. ▶

You may need to _____ on some of the information in your presentation if

your classmates _____ .

Our Turn

Discuss
Listen
Write

Read the prompt. Work with the teacher to complete the frames. Write a thoughtful response that includes a convincing reason. ▶

PROMPT: **How could you elaborate on a description of your school?**

To _____ on a description of my school, I could focus on the places where

students spend the most time, such as the library and the _____ .

Then, I could add some details about the _____

and _____ .

Be an Academic Author

Write
Discuss
Listen

Read the prompt and complete the frames. Strengthen your response with a relevant example.

PROMPT: **What could you do to elaborate on the sentence "*The man drove a car.*" ?**

To _____ on this sentence, I could add specific information

about _____ and the type of car. For example:

The gray haired man drove his rusty old _____ *slowly to the*

_____ .

Construct a Response

Write
Discuss
Listen

Read the prompt and construct a thoughtful response. Include a valid reason to strengthen your response.

PROMPT: **Think about your favorite activity. If you were asked to elaborate on why you like it, what would you say?**

_____

_____

_____

_____

grammar tip ▶

A **common noun** names any person, place, thing, or idea. **Plural nouns** name more than one person, place, thing, or idea. The words *some* and *the* often appear before a plural noun.

EXAMPLE: In *the* Arctic regions of Canada, *some* Inuit people still live in houses made of snow and ice.

present

DAY 1

REVIEW: prior *adjective*

_____ to the predicted storm, people in my neighborhood

prepared by _____ .

DAY 2

present *verb*

One way to clearly _____ your history

project is to create a poster that includes _____ .

DAY 3

When you are _____ a poem to the class, you should

speak _____ so that everyone can follow along easily.

DAY 4

After I won the spelling contest, the teacher _____ me

with (a/an) _____ _____ .

DAY 5

Next week, I have to _____ my short story in front of the

class, and I feel _____ .

TOTAL

96

🏁 **SMART** START

DAY 1

REVIEW: present   *verb*

Yesterday at the school assembly, the principal _____

three _____

to the students who sold the most raffle tickets for the school fundraiser.

☐
☐

DAY 2

develop   *verb*

Over the weekend, I _____

an idea for a video about our school's new _____ .

So today I will present my idea to our principal.

☐
☐

DAY 3

I am _____ my math skills by

_____ every day.

☐
☐

DAY 4

The city supervisors have to _____ a plan for the new

_____ before they can begin building.

☐
☐

DAY 5

It took many years for the author to _____ her ideas

about an old, _____ into a successful mystery novel.

☐
☐

TOTAL

provide

SMART**SMART**START

DAY 1

REVIEW: **develop**   *verb*

A rowdy puppy _____ into a helpful

_____ with proper training.

DAY 2

provide   *verb*

I can _____ you with a map that shows the way to the

_____ .

DAY 3

During our recent trip to the art museum, the guide _____

us with interesting information about the _____ on display .

DAY 4

Most of my teachers _____ helpful feedback when they

check my _____ .

DAY 5

Today the music director is going to _____ a rehearsal schedule

for the chorus so they will be ready to sing at the _____ .

TOTAL

SMART START

REVIEW: provide   *verb*

Who will _____ our class with

_____ for the science fair group projects?

□
□

revise   *verb*

My family and I _____ the plans for our

_____ because my grandmother became very ill.

□
□

I had to _____ the invitation to my birthday party

because the _____ was incorrect.

□
□

At their meeting yesterday, the junior youth group _____

their plan for the summer party because they need more _____

_____ .

□
□

One thing I usually have to correct when I am _____

a first draft is my _____ .

□
□

TOTAL

demonstrate

REVIEW: revise *verb*

DAY 1

Yesterday, my sister helped me _____ my final draft by

finding _____ that I hadn't noticed.

☐
☐

---

demonstrate *verb*

DAY 2

At the Natural History Museum, a Native American artist _____

how to make _____ .

☐
☐

DAY 3

By pointing to the map during social studies last week, I _____

that I understood the location of _____ .

☐
☐

DAY 4

My cousin's large vocabulary and knowledge of many topics such as

_____ clearly _____

the benefits of reading daily.

☐
☐

DAY 5

I can _____ that I'm responsible by

_____ when I'm at home.

☐
☐

TOTAL

SMART START

DAY 1

REVIEW: demonstrate   *verb*

In gym class yesterday, our new classmate _____ his

ability to _____ .

☐
☐

DAY 2

elaborate   *verb*

The police officer asked the woman to _____ on her

description of the _____ .

☐
☐

DAY 3

If your report is too short and too general, you need to _____

by adding more _____ .

☐
☐

DAY 4

I asked the teacher to _____

on her directions for our _____

assignment because it wasn't clear to me the first time.

☐
☐

DAY 5

I wanted to know the real reason my friend _____ ,

so I asked him to _____ on the reason he gave.

☐
☐

TOTAL

Compare and Contrast

To **compare** two or more things analyze what is the same.

To **contrast** two or more things analyze what is different.

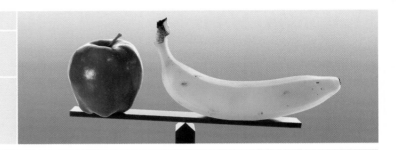

 Find It   **Compare** apples and bananas and circle what is the same.

Apples and Bananas

- are sweet

- grow on underground

- are white inside

 Try It   **Contrast** what is different about apples and bananas by adding ideas to each list.

Apples	Bananas
• have a smooth surface you can eat	• must be peeled to eat
• have a slightly round shape	• have long shape
• are _____	• are _____

RATE WORD KNOWLEDGE

Circle the number that shows your knowledge of the words you'll use to compare and contrast.

3rd Grade	BEFORE	4th Grade	AFTER	5th Grade
		RATE IT		
alike	1 2 3 4	**similar**	1 2 3 4	comparison
different	1 2 3 4	**difference**	1 2 3 4	comparable
similar	1 2 3 4	**similarity**	1 2 3 4	contrast
difference	1 2 3 4	**differently**	1 2 3 4	identical
similarity	1 2 3 4	**common**	1 2 3 4	unique
opposite	1 2 3 4	**unlike**	1 2 3 4	differ

DISCUSSION GUIDE
- Form groups of four.
- Assign letters to each person.
- Each group member takes a turn leading a discussion.
- Prepare to report about one word.

Ⓐ Ⓑ
Ⓓ Ⓒ

DISCUSS WORDS

Discuss how well you know the fourth grade words. Then, report to the class how you rated each word.

GROUP LEADER **Ask**

So, _____ what do you know
(NAME)

about the word _____ ?

GROUP MEMBERS **Discuss**

1 = I **don't recognize** the word _____ .

I need to learn what it means.

2 = I **recognize** the word _____ ,

but I need to learn the meaning.

3 = I'm **familiar** with the word _____ .

I think it means _____ .

4 = I **know** the word _____ .

It's a _____ , and it means _____ .
(PART OF SPEECH)

Here is my example sentence: _____ .

REPORTER **Report Word Knowledge**

Our group gave the word _____ a rating of _____ because _____ .

SET A GOAL AND REFLECT

First, set a vocabulary goal for this unit by selecting at least three words that you plan to thoroughly learn. At the end of the unit, return to this page and write a reflection about one word you have mastered.

GOAL

During this unit I plan to thoroughly learn the words _____ ,

_____ , and _____ . Increasing my word knowledge will

help me speak and write effectively when I compare and _____ .

As a result of this unit, I feel most confident about the word _____ .

This is my model sentence: _____

_____ .

REFLECTION

similar

adjective

 Write it: _____ **Write it again:** _____

 _____

TOOLKIT

Meaning almost the same	**Examples** • The flags of Colombia and Ecuador are **similar** because they have the same three _____ . 
Synonyms • like; alike **Antonyms** • different; dissimilar	• Our dog and our neighbor's dog are **similar** because they are both the same _____ . 

Family
• **Noun:** similarity
• **Adverb:** similarly

Word Partners
• similar to

• a similar appearance

Examples
• A lemon is **similar to** a lime because they have the same shape, and they are both sour-tasting citrus fruits.
• Our French Bulldog and our neighbor's Boston Terrier have **a similar appearance**, because they both have pointed ears.

 Try It

My taste in music is **similar** to my sister's. We both like _____ music.

VERBAL PRACTICE

Talk about it   Discuss ideas with your partner, listen to classmates, and then write your favorite idea.

Discuss
Listen
Write

1. Some of our classmates are wearing **similar** _____ today.

2. When I look at old family photos, I notice that my _____

   and I have a **similar** appearance.

WRITING PRACTICE

Collaborate

Discuss
Agree
Write
Listen

Discuss ideas with your partner and agree on the best words to complete the frame. ▶

Third graders and fourth graders may have a _____ appearance, but in

reality, most fourth graders are _____ than third graders.

Our Turn

Discuss
Listen
Write

Read the prompt. Work with the teacher to complete the frames. Write a thoughtful response that includes a personal experience. ▶

PROMPT: How important is it to you to have friends with similar interests?

It's great to have friends with interests that are _____ to mine, but it's also important

for us to develop our own special interests. For example, I have a close friend who likes to

_____ , just like me. However, (he/she) _____

also enjoys playing with _____ , but I don't find that interesting.

Be an Academic Author

Write
Discuss
Listen

Read the prompt and complete the frames. Strengthen your response with a relevant example. ▶

PROMPT: Think about two movie actors that are similar in some way. How are they alike?

The movie actor _____ is _____ in some ways

to the actor _____ . For example, they both have

_____ and act in movies that feature _____

_____ .

Construct a Response

Write
Discuss
Listen

Read the prompt and construct a thoughtful response. Include relevant examples to strengthen your response. ▶

PROMPT: Think about two relatives who have similar qualities (for example: cooking ability, sense of humor, tardiness, etc.) Describe how they are similar and how they are different.

_____

_____

_____

_____

grammar tip ▶

Adjectives are always singular even if they describe a plural noun. Do not add an **-s** to adjectives that describe plural nouns.

EXAMPLE: Monarch butterflies are identified by their *orange* and *black* wings.

difference

noun

Write it: _____   **Write it again:** _____

_____

TOOLKIT

Meaning
how one thing is not like another

Synonyms
• not alike

Antonyms
• same

Examples

One **difference** between some male and female birds is the color of their _____ .

• Learning about and celebrating cultural **differences** can strengthen a _____ .

Forms
• **Singular:** difference
• **Plural:** differences

Family
• **Verb:** differ
• **Adjective:** different
• **Adverb:** differently

Word Partners
• a/the/one difference between _____ and _____ (two or more items)
• a **major** difference (in/ between)

Examples
• **One difference between** sneakers and flip flops is that one has shoelaces.

• If you don't get enough sleep, you will notice **a major difference in** your ability to focus at school.

 Try It

One **difference** between my older sister and me is that she is _____ and I am not.

VERBAL PRACTICE

Talk about it   Discuss ideas with your partner, listen to classmates, and then write your favorite idea.

Discuss
Listen
Write

1. The biggest **difference** between going to school and being on vacation is the amount of

   time I'm able to spend _____ during the summer.

2. There are some major **differences** in the types of _____

   that adults and children enjoy.

difference

noun

WRITING PRACTICE

Collaborate

Discuss
Agree
Write
Listen

Discuss ideas with your partner and agree on the best words to complete the frame. ▶

Two major _____ between deserts and (a/an) _____ _____

are the amount of water and the types of _____ present.

Our Turn

Discuss
Listen
Write

Read the prompt. Work with the teacher to complete the frames. Write a thoughtful response that includes a convincing reason. ▶
PROMPT: Think about one subject that you enjoy in school, and one you dislike. What is one difference between the two subjects?

One school subject that I enjoy is _____ , and one that I dislike is

_____ . One _____ between the two is that in the

first class, I prefer learning how to _____ , but in

the second class I dislike how we often have to _____ a lot.

Be an Academic Author

Write
Discuss
Listen

Read the prompt and complete the frames. Strengthen your response with a relevant example. ▶
PROMPT: What is an obvious difference between a movie and a novel?

An obvious _____ between a movie and a novel is that movies show viewers

_____ that you can only imagine when reading. For example,

the novel _____ was made into a movie.

Instead of reading about the location of _____

_____ , I could see it on the screen.

Construct a Response

Write
Discuss
Listen

Read the prompt and construct a thoughtful response. Include a convincing reason to strengthen your response. ▶
PROMPT: Think about one job you might enjoy as an adult and one job you would not enjoy. What is the difference between them, and why do you prefer one over the other?

_____

_____

_____

grammar tip ▶

Count nouns name things that can be counted. Count nouns have two forms, singular and plural. To make most count nouns plural, add **-s**. To make count nouns that end in *x, ch, sh, ss,* and *z* plural, add **-es**.

EXAMPLE: Red *foxes* live around the world in many diverse *habitats*.

similarity

noun

Say it: sim • i • la • ri • ty

Write it: _____   **Write it again:** _____

_____

TOOLKIT

Meaning
a likeness or sameness

Examples
- When the _____ stand together, it's easy to see the **similarities** between them.

Synonyms
- resemblance

Antonyms
- difference

- One **similarity** that Earth and Venus share is that they are about the same _____ .

EARTH   VENUS

Forms
- **Singular:** similarity
- **Plural:** similarities

Family
- **Adjective:** similar
- **Adverb:** similarly

Word Partners
- (a/the) similarity between
- one similarity ____ shares with ____ is

Examples
- **A similarity between** you and me is that we are both in 4th grade.
- **One similarity** my cousin **shares with** me **is** that we are both girls.

Try It
One **similarity** between a moth and a butterfly is that they both _____ .

VERBAL PRACTICE

Talk about it   Discuss ideas with your partner, listen to classmates, and then write your favorite idea.

Discuss
Listen
Write

1. Pineapples and _____ share a few **similarities**. They are both large, juicy, and _____ fruits.

2. One **similarity** between apes, such as chimpanzees, and humans is that we can both _____ .

WRITING PRACTICE

Collaborate
Discuss
Agree
Write
Listen

Discuss ideas with your partner and agree on the best words to complete the frame. ▶

The popular games _____ and Apples to Apples share some _____ ,

such as taking turns and _____ to win.

Our Turn
Discuss
Listen
Write

Read the prompt. Work with the teacher to complete the frames. Write a thoughtful response that includes a personal experience. ▶

PROMPT: **Think about a fictional character in a book you read (or in a movie you saw) that you felt a strong connection to. What is one similarity between you and this character?**

A fictional character I felt a strong connection to is _____ from the

(book/movie) _____ _____ .

One _____ between this character and me is that we are

both _____ when confronting difficult situations in our lives.

Be an Academic Author
Write
Discuss
Listen

Read the prompt and complete the frames. Strengthen your response with a relevant example. ▶

PROMPT: **Think of two popular singers you know. What are some similarities between them?**

There are several _____ between the singers _____

and _____ . For example, they are both famous

_____ singers who _____ extremely well.

Construct a Response
Write
Discuss
Listen

Read the prompt and construct a thoughtful response. Include relevant examples to strengthen your response. ▶

PROMPT: **Compare your bedroom with a friend's or sibling's bedroom. Describe at least two similarities.**

_____

_____

_____

_____

grammar tip ▶

Count nouns name things that can be counted. Count nouns have two forms, singular and plural. When count nouns end in a consonant + *-y*, drop the *y* and add *-ies*.

EXAMPLE: Ants and bees live in *colonies*.

differently
adverb

 Write it: _____ **Write it again:** _____

 _____

Meaning	**Examples**
in a different way; in another way	• People from different cultures often _____ **differently**. 
Synonyms	• The special television _____ made me think **differently** about animal shelters. 
• another way	
Antonyms	
• similarly	

Family
- **Noun:** difference
- **Adjective:** different

Word Partners
- act/react differently

- _____ (verb: think, walk, talk) differently

Examples
- Although my father laughed at my joke, I felt worried when my mother **reacted differently** and frowned.
- People from different regions of the same country often **talk differently**.

 Try It

My friends **act differently** in class than they do when we are _____ at recess.

VERBAL PRACTICE

Talk about it

Discuss
Listen
Write

Discuss ideas with your partner, listen to classmates, and then write your favorite idea.

1. If you're going to a relative's wedding, you need to dress **differently** than if you're going to

_____.

2. Our science teacher demonstrates how one liquid reacts **differently** when it

_____ other substances.

WRITING PRACTICE

Collaborate

Discuss
Agree
Write
Listen

Discuss ideas with your partner and agree on the best words to complete the frame. ▶

Young children behave _____ than older children. For example, many toddlers

_____ when they can't have something. However, older

children usually act more _____ .

Our Turn

Discuss
Listen
Write

Read the prompt. Work with the teacher to complete the frames. Write a thoughtful response that includes a convincing reason. ▶

PROMPT: What adults do you speak to differently than you do to your friends and why?

I speak _____ to my _____ than I do

to my friends. This is because it's acceptable to joke and speak casually with friends.

However, with adults it is important to be more _____ and use

_____ vocabulary.

Be an Academic Author

Write
Discuss
Listen

Read the prompt and complete the frames. Strengthen your response with a relevant example. ▶

PROMPT: Imagine that you tried out for a singing and dancing competition and you didn't do well, but they invited you for a second audition. What could you do differently to perform better?

If I tried out for a competition but performed _____ , I would do

several things _____ to prepare for the second audition. For example, I could

start _____ much earlier.

Construct a Response

Write
Discuss
Listen

Read the prompt and construct a thoughtful response. Include a relevant example to strengthen your response. ▶

PROMPT: Describe a time you did something that you regretted or felt bad about. How will you act differently if you are ever in the same situation again?

_____

_____

_____

grammar tip ▶

An **adverb** describes an action. Adverbs usually end in **-ly** and come after the verb to describe how the action is done.

EXAMPLE: When we won the game, everyone cheered *loudly*.

in common
noun

Say it: com • mon

 Write it: _____ **Write it again:** _____

 _____

TOOLKIT

Meaning
having features that are alike or the same

Examples
- One feature that puppies and baby rabbits have **in common** is soft, fluffy _____ .

Synonyms
- shared; same

- My sister and her friends have long _____ **in common** with each other.

Forms
- **Singular:** common
- **Plural:** common

Word Partners
- in common with
- have (things/something nothing) in common

Examples
- What traits do you have **in common with** your brother or sister?
- A horse and a tree **have nothing in common**.

Try It
My mother and I have several physical traits **in common**, such as the shape of our _____ .

VERBAL PRACTICE

Talk about it

Discuss
Listen
Write

Discuss ideas with your partner, listen to classmates, and then write your favorite idea.

1. One trait that house cats have **in common** with tigers is that they both like _____

_____ .

2. One feature that butterflies have **in common** with _____ is that they both fly.

in common

noun

WRITING PRACTICE

Collaborate

Discuss
Agree
Write
Listen

Discuss ideas with your partner and agree on the best words to complete the frame. ▶

Many summer camps provide young people with opportunities to explore art and

_____ , and to discover that they have some interests in

_____ with other students.

Our Turn

Discuss
Listen
Write

Read the prompt. Work with the teacher to complete the frames. Write a thoughtful response that includes a convincing reason.

PROMPT: **What is an interest that you and your best friend have in common?**

One thing my best friend and I have in _____ is our interest in

_____ . We often enjoy _____

_____ together on weekends or during vacations.

Be an Academic Author

Write
Discuss
Listen

Read the prompt and complete the frames. Strengthen your response with a relevant example. ▶

PROMPT: **Soccer and hockey may seem to have little in common, but they actually share several common features. Explain some features that soccer has in common with hockey.**

Soccer and hockey seem very different, but they actually have several features in _____ .

For example, both sports have several _____ , and both teams have the

objective to _____ move a ball or puck into a net to score a goal.

Construct a Response

Write
Discuss
Listen

Read the prompt and construct a thoughtful response. Include a valid reason to strengthen your response. ▶

PROMPT: **Sometimes it is hard to see what we have in common with someone we just met. Describe a time when you realized that you had more in common with someone than you originally thought.**

_____

_____

_____

_____

grammar tip ▶

Quantity adjectives tell "how much" or "how many." Quantity adjectives go before a plural noun. Common quantity adjectives are: *most, many, some, several, both.*

EXAMPLE: *Most* people have *many* things to consider before making the decision to adopt a pet.

unlike
preposition

 Write it: _____ **Write it again:** _____

_____

TOOLKIT

Meaning	Examples
different; not the same	• Living in a big city is **unlike** living in the _____ in many ways. 
Synonyms • different; not alike **Antonyms** • like; alike; similar	• **Unlike** a roller coaster, a water slide ends with a huge _____ .

Word Partners

• Unlike _____

• _____ is unlike some/many/ most/other _____

Examples

• **Unlike** my friends, who take the bus, I ride my bike to school.
• This cake **is unlike most other** cakes because it is sugar-free.

 Try It

Unlike sharks, dolphins are _____ mammals.

VERBAL PRACTICE

Talk about it

Discuss
Listen
Write

Discuss ideas with your partner, listen to classmates, and then write your favorite idea.

1. Swimming in a pool is **unlike** swimming in the ocean because there (isn't/aren't any) _____ _____ in a pool.

2. **Unlike** a lemon, a banana is very _____ .

WRITING PRACTICE

Collaborate

Discuss
Agree
Write
Listen

Discuss ideas with your partner and agree on the best words to complete the frame. ▶

Kindergarteners are _____ fourth-graders because they spend most school

days doing short, fun-filled activities like _____

rather than solving math problems and learning new vocabulary.

Our Turn

Discuss
Listen
Write

Read the prompt. Work with the teacher to complete the frames. Write a thoughtful response that includes a convincing reason. ▶

PROMPT: Think about someone you know who is completely unlike anyone else you've ever met. What makes this person unique?

My _____ is completely _____ most people I know. This is because

(he/she) _____ is a very _____ person who loves to

_____ .

Be an Academic Author

Write
Discuss
Listen

Read the prompt and complete the frames. Strengthen your response with a relevant example. ▶

PROMPT: Although cars and motorcycles are both forms of transportation, they are unlike each other in many ways. Explain one way in which cars and motorcycles are unlike each other.

One way in which cars are _____ motorcycles is that most cars have

_____ while motorcycles do not. This makes cars

_____ than motorcycles.

Construct a Response

Write
Discuss
Listen

Read the prompt and construct a thoughtful response. Include relevant examples to strengthen your response.

PROMPT: Sometimes siblings, or even friends, can be completely unlike one another. Explain how you are unlike your brother, sister, or one of your friends.

_____

_____

_____

_____

grammar tip ▶

Quantity adjectives tell "how much" or "how many." Quantity adjectives go before a plural noun. Common quantity adjectives are: *most, many, some, several, both.*

EXAMPLE: *Some* groups worked on their projects over *several* days.

similar

DAY 1	**REVIEW:** elaborate *verb*

When I did not understand the plans for the party, my best friend

_____ on how to do the make-your-own

_____ party activity.

DAY 2	**similar** *adjective*

Cookies are _____ to cupcakes in that they are both

_____ treats.

DAY 3

Some poisonous and non-poisonous _____ may have a

_____ appearance, but an experienced outdoor explorer can

tell them apart.

DAY 4

Painting and _____ are _____

activities in that they both require creativity and imagination.

DAY 5

Among all my family members, I am most _____ to my

_____ because we both like to watch funny movies.

TOTAL

116

SMART START

DAY 1

REVIEW: similar *adjective*

Frogs are _____ to toads in that they both

_____ .

☐
☐

difference *noun*

DAY 2

There is a huge _____ between the food I eat at

_____ and the food I eat at home.

☐
☐

DAY 3

A major _____ between reptiles and fish is that reptiles

have _____ , while fish have fins.

☐
☐

DAY 4

If you travel to another country, you might notice some _____

in the way people _____ .

☐
☐

DAY 5

One major _____ between an ocean and a lake is that an

ocean has _____ .

☐
☐

TOTAL

similarity

DAY 1

REVIEW: difference   *noun*

One major _____ between outdoor sports and video game

sports is that outdoor sports require much more _____ .

☐
☐

DAY 2

similarity   *noun*

One _____ between Venezuela and

_____ is that they are both Spanish-speaking countries.

☐
☐

DAY 3

A _____ between running and swimming is that they are

both _____ activities.

☐
☐

DAY 4

Hair color is one _____ I share with my

_____ .

☐
☐

DAY 5

There are a few _____ between my science and social

studies books: both textbooks have colorful images and difficult

_____ .

☐
☐

TOTAL

SMART START

DAY 1

REVIEW: similarity   *noun*

One _____ between coffee and tea is that they are both

_____ .

DAY 2

differently   *adverb*

I walk _____ on ice than I do on

_____ .

DAY 3

A dog will react to you very _____ if you seem

_____ than if you are calm and relaxed.

DAY 4

Bicycles and _____ are both forms of transportation, but

they work very _____ .

DAY 5

One way in which my friends and I think _____ is that many

of them enjoy _____ , but I do not.

TOTAL

in common

DAY 1

REVIEW: **differently**   *adverb*

Many kids try hard to fit in with their _____ ,

but kids should also be proud of the ways in which they dress, think, and do things

_____ .

☐
☐

in common   *noun*

DAY 2

Oceans and lakes have some things in _____ . For example,

they are both places where you can _____ .

☐
☐

DAY 3

Action adventures and magazine articles don't have very much in _____ ,

but I prefer reading them more than doing _____ .

☐
☐

DAY 4

Identical twins usually have a lot in _____ , such as the same

_____ .

☐
☐

DAY 5

Rectangles have some features in _____ with squares. For

example, they both have _____ .

☐
☐

TOTAL

 **SMART** *START*

DAY 1

REVIEW: in common   *noun*

One thing that all species of birds have in _____ is that they

all have _____ .

☐

☐

DAY 2

unlike   *preposition*

_____ parrots, penguins can't

_____ .

☐

☐

DAY 3

Ice cream is _____ a cookie because ice cream is cold and

creamy, and cookies are _____ .

☐

☐

DAY 4

I don't enjoy _____ 's music,

_____ many of my classmates.

☐

☐

DAY 5

I am always respectful to my _____ ,

_____ some people my age.

☐

☐

TOTAL

Inference

To make an **inference** use a picture or information from text and what we already know to form an idea.

 Find It Look at the picture above. Answer each question and make an **inference**.

What do you already know? +	**What has happened in the picture?**	= **My inference**
I already know that some schools close when it <u>snows</u>.	The storm has covered the buses with _____.	I think the schools will be _____.

 Try It Read the headline from the newspaper. Answer each question and make an **inference**.

THE FLU SEASON HITS 30 PEOPLE

What do you already know? +	**What does the headline mean?**	= **My inference**
I already know that the flu is a _____.	The headline means that many people are sick with the _____.	So this means I should wash my hands often and avoid people who seem _____.

RATE WORD KNOWLEDGE

Rate how well you know Toolkit words you'll use when you make inferences.

3rd Grade	BEFORE	4th Grade	AFTER	5th Grade
decide	1 2 3 4	**conclude**	1 2 3 4	interpret
predict	1 2 3 4	**assume**	1 2 3 4	infer
figure out	1 2 3 4	**conclusion**	1 2 3 4	deduce
probably	1 2 3 4	**assumption**	1 2 3 4	context
clue	1 2 3 4	**determine**	1 2 3 4	presume
prediction	1 2 3 4	**communicate**	1 2 3 4	imply

DISCUSSION GUIDE
- Form groups of four.
- Assign letters to each person.
- Each group member takes a turn leading a discussion.
- Prepare to report about one word.

Ⓐ Ⓑ
Ⓓ Ⓒ

DISCUSS WORDS

Discuss how well you know the fourth grade words. Then, report to the class how you rated each word.

GROUP LEADER **Ask**

So, _____ what do you know
(NAME)

about the word _____ ?

GROUP MEMBERS **Discuss**

1 = I **don't recognize** the word _____ .

I need to learn what it means.

2 = I **recognize** the word _____ ,

but I need to learn the meaning.

3 = I'm **familiar** with the word _____ .

I think it means _____ .

4 = I **know** the word _____ .

It's a _____ , and it means _____ .
(PART OF SPEECH)

Here is my example sentence: _____ .

REPORTER **Report Word Knowledge**

Our group gave the word _____ a rating of _____ because _____ .

SET A GOAL AND REFLECT

First, set a vocabulary goal for this unit by selecting at least three words that you plan to thoroughly learn. At the end of the unit, return to this page and write a reflection about one word you have mastered.

GOAL

During this unit I plan to thoroughly learn the words _____ ,

_____ , and _____ . Increasing my word knowledge will

help me speak and write effectively when I make an _____ .

As a result of this unit, I feel most confident about the word _____ .

This is my model sentence: _____

REFLECTION

_____ .

conclude
verb

Say it: con • clude

 Write it: _____   **Write it again:** _____

 _____

TOOLKIT

Meaning	Examples
to decide something is factual or true after looking carefully at information	• After seeing her expression, I **concluded** that my cousin was _____ about her gift.

Synonyms
• decide; think

• On Sunday I often read the weather forecast so I can **conclude** what to wear to _____ during the week.

Mo Thu We Th Fr Sa Su

Forms
• **Present:**
  I/You/We/They   conclude
  He/She/It   concludes
• **Past:** concluded

Family
• **Noun:** conclusion

Word Partners
• conclude that
• conclude from _____ that

Examples
• When the baby cries, my aunt **concludes that** the baby is hungry.
• I can **conclude from** the loud music next door **that** my neighbor's son is practicing with his rock band.

 Try It

If you see an open garbage can and _____ scattered all around, you might **conclude** that a racoon raided the trash.

VERBAL PRACTICE

Talk about it   Discuss ideas with your partner, listen to classmates, and then write your favorite idea.

Discuss
Listen
Write

1. If you receive a message that your mother will be home late, you can **conclude** that you

   need to _____ .

2. When no one from our school received an award at the science fair, the principal **concluded**

   that we needed new _____ .

WRITING PRACTICE

Collaborate
Discuss
Agree
Write
Listen

Discuss ideas with your partner and agree on the best words to complete the frame. ▶

After discovering that the _____ had disappeared from the

kitchen counter, my uncle could _____ that his dog had eaten it all.

Our Turn
Discuss
Listen
Write

Read the prompt. Work with the teacher to complete the frames. Write a thoughtful response that includes a relevant example. ▶

PROMPT: If students started bringing bag lunches after the cafeteria stopped serving pizza, what could you conclude about this menu change?

We could _____ that pizza is a popular menu item. So, we

would recommend that the cafeteria staff serve _____ and

_____ pizzas on Tuesdays and Thursdays.

Be an Academic Author
Write
Discuss
Listen

Read the prompt and complete the frames. Strengthen your response with a convincing reason.

PROMPT: A dog always barks when his owner leaves the room. What can you conclude about the dog? What would you recommend?

I can _____ that the dog does not like to be alone. One reason

the dog barks might be to _____.

I would recommend that his owner leave (a/an) _____ _____

with the dog when he leaves.

Construct a Response
Write
Discuss
Listen

Read the prompt and construct a thoughtful response. Include a relevant example to strengthen your response. ▶

PROMPT: Usually, when a team wins a game, people cheer, clap, and hug their friends. What could you conclude from a crowd that is walking quietly and slowly after a game?

_____

_____

_____

_____

grammar tip ▶

Use the modal verb, or helping verb *could* to show that something might be possible. When you use *could*, add a verb in the base form.

EXAMPLE: To let your parents/guardians know that you got home safely, you *could* text or call them at work.

assume
verb

 Write it: _____   **Write it again:** _____

 _____

TOOLKIT

Meaning to think that something is probably true	**Examples** • We can **assume** that the runner is _____ because her hand is on the base. 
Synonyms • think; guess **Antonyms** • prove	• I **assumed** that my sister had heard the news but when I saw her expression I knew she was very _____ . 

Forms
- **Present:**
  I/You/We/They   assume
  He/She/It   assumes
- **Past:** assumed

Family
- **Noun:** assumption

Word Partners
- (I/you/he/she/we) can/can't assume that
- assume from _____ that

Examples
- Just because he isn't smiling, **you can't assume that** your friend is unhappy.
- We **assumed from** the dark house **that** our friends weren't home.

 Try It

My mom was so excited after seeing the commercial for the new _____ ,
I **assumed** that she would buy it right away.

VERBAL PRACTICE

Talk about it

Discuss
Listen
Write

Discuss ideas with your partner, listen to classmates, and then write your favorite idea.

1. My sister worked on _____ every day for the

   entire summer, so we all **assumed** that she would easily win an award at the competition.

2. When preparing for an important history test, you should always **assume** that there will

   be at least one _____ question.

WRITING PRACTICE

Collaborate

Discuss
Agree
Write
Listen

Discuss ideas with your partner and agree on the best words to complete the frame. ▶

After we noticed a moving van parked in front of the house next door, we _____

that our neighbors would soon be moving to _____ .

Our Turn

Discuss
Listen
Write

Read the prompt. Work with the teacher to complete the frames. Write a thoughtful response that includes a relevant example. ▶

PROMPT: Most computer games have several levels of difficulty. What can you assume if you master one level of a computer game?

If you master one level of difficulty of a computer game, you can _____

that the next level will be more _____ . For example, in the computer

games we've played, the higher levels give players new _____ to solve.

Be an Academic Author

Write
Discuss
Listen

Read the prompt and complete the frames. Strengthen your response with a convincing reason. ▶

PROMPT: Many people who are allergic to peanuts read food labels that say the equipment that prepared the product was also used to process nuts. What would you assume from this information and why is it important?

If a label says that the equipment was also used to process nuts, I would _____

that the food might contain peanuts. This is important because people who are allergic

could _____ after eating foods with peanuts.

Construct a Response

Write
Discuss
Listen

Read the prompt and construct a thoughtful response. Include a convincing reason to strengthen your response. ▶

PROMPT: A recent report showed that children who drink sugary beverages often develop illnesses. What would you assume from reading this report and why is it important?

_____

_____

_____

_____

grammar tip ▶

A **past-tense verb** describes an action that already happened. For verbs that end in silent *e*, drop the final *e* before you add **-ed**.

EXAMPLE: Last weekend, my aunt and I **baked** a chocolate cake with sprinkles and **saved** a slice for my friend.

conclusion
noun

Say it: con • clu • sion

 Write it: _____   **Write it again:** _____

 _____

TOOLKIT

Meaning
a decision you make or an idea you have

Examples
- The sisters reached a **conclusion** about which picture to _____ to their dad.

Synonyms
- judgment; decision

- My science partner agreed with my **conclusion** that the _____ contained pollen.

Forms
- **Singular:** conclusion
- **Plural:** conclusions

Family
- **Verb:** conclude

Word Partners
- came to the conclusion that

- draw a/the conclusion

Examples
- After searching for many hours, my mother **came to the conclusion** that she had lost her cell phone.

- Because the woman told me not to pet her dog, I **drew the conclusion** that the dog was dangerous.

 Try It
After waiting at the stop light for more than five minutes, the _____
driver **concluded** that the traffic light was not working properly.

VERBAL PRACTICE

Talk about it

Discuss
Listen
Write

Discuss ideas with your partner, listen to classmates, and then write your favorite idea.

1. For our cooking project, we thought making _____ would be easy but after trying, we came to the **conclusion** that they were very difficult to make.

2. After seeing my little sister's mad expression, I drew the **conclusion** that she was angry that I ate the last _____ .

conclusion

noun

WRITING PRACTICE

Collaborate

Discuss
Agree
Write
Listen

Discuss ideas with your partner and agree on the best words to complete the frame. ▷

After reading two different reviews of the upcoming movie, we came to the _____

that the movie would be _____ for kids under 10.

Our Turn

Discuss
Listen
Write

Read the prompt. Work with the teacher to complete the frames. Write a thoughtful response that includes a relevant example. ▷

PROMPT: How would your class reach a conclusion about where to go on a field trip?

To plan a field trip, our class would first discuss _____ places to visit.

For example, we could visit the _____ . Then, we would

vote to come to a _____ about where to go.

Be an Academic Author

Write
Discuss
Listen

Read the prompt and complete the frames. Strengthen your response with a relevant example. ▷

PROMPT: A study found that children who were responsible pet owners often become caring professionals later in life. What conclusion can you draw about the study?

According to the study, having to _____ a pet teaches

young children responsibility. So, I can easily draw the _____

that it is _____ for a child to own a pet.

Construct a Response

Write
Discuss
Listen

Read the prompt and construct a thoughtful response. Include a relevant example to strengthen your response. ▷

PROMPT: A magazine article reported that many young video gamers are able to draw detailed pictures and tell creative stories. What conclusion can you draw from this article?

_____

_____

_____

_____

---

grammar tip ▷

Count nouns name things that can be counted. Count nouns have a singular form and a plural form. To make most count nouns plural, add **-s**. To make count nouns that end in *x, ch, sh, ss,* and *z*, plural, add **-es**.

EXAMPLE: *Hours* of research taught me that *cockatoos* are smart *birds*.

assumption

noun

Say it: as • **sump** • tion

 Write it: _____   **Write it again:** _____

 _____

TOOLKIT

Meaning
an idea you have about something that is not always true

Synonyms
• guess

Examples
• Seeing the dogs play for hours, I made the **assumption** they _____ each other.

• When my cousins arrived with balloons, I made the **assumption** that they knew it was my _____ .

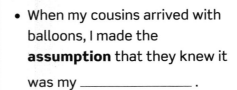

Forms
• **Singular:** assumption
• **Plural:** assumptions

Family
• **Verb:** assume

Word Partners
• (my/your/his/her/our) assumption is that
• make an/the (false) assumption

Examples
• In the morning, when I hear the beep of the school intercom, **my assumption is that** the principal will make the daily announcement.
• Seeing the school bus drive away without my sister onboard, it is easy to **make the assumption** that she overslept again.

Try It
Even though I had no cavities at my last check-up, my dentist told me not to make the **assumption** that I did not need to _____ regularly.

VERBAL PRACTICE

Talk about it

Discuss ideas with your partner, listen to classmates, and then write your favorite idea.

Discuss
Listen
Write

1. Some people make the false **assumption** that all pit bull dogs are _____

   _____ .

2. If you see a long line at the movie theater, you can make an **assumption** that you (will/will not) _____ _____ .

WRITING PRACTICE

Collaborate

Discuss
Agree
Write
Listen

Discuss ideas with your partner and agree on the best words to complete the frame. ▶

When you are riding your bike, it is very _____ to make an

_____ that a car will always stop for you at an intersection.

Our Turn

Discuss
Listen
Write

Read the prompt. Work with the teacher to complete the frames. Write a thoughtful response that includes a convincing reason. ▶

PROMPT: During spring, when someone sneezes, many people make the assumption that the person has the flu. Why is it a bad idea to make this assumption?

When people sneeze, my _____ is that they have the flu.

However, this may be a false **assumption** because they might just have an allergy due to

_____ .

Be an Academic Author

Write
Discuss
Listen

Read the prompt and complete the frames. Strengthen your response with a convincing reason. ▶

PROMPT: If you saw a high school boy helping an elderly person in the grocery store, what assumption would you make about him?

If I saw a high school boy helping an elderly person I would make the _____

that he has (a/an) _____ _____ character. I would assume that

he believes it is important to _____ senior citizens.

Construct a Response

Write
Discuss
Listen

Read the prompt and construct a thoughtful response. Include a convincing reason to strengthen your response. ▶

PROMPT: If you saw a movie with a new friend, and when it was over she tried to convince you to sneak into another show without paying, what assumption would you make and how would you react?

_____

_____

_____

_____

grammar tip ▶

An **adjective** describes, or tells about, a noun. An adjective sometimes appears after verbs such as *is, are, look, feel, smell,* and *taste.*

EXAMPLE: My dad told us to empty the garbage because it smelled *rotten* and *disgusting*.

determine
verb

 Write it: _____ **Write it again:** _____

 _____

TOOLKIT

Meaning	Examples
to decide; to conclude	• The best way to **determine** if you like the _____ for the cake is to taste it.
Synonyms • figure out	• My teacher used a weather app on his phone to **determine** which day would be ideal for the _____ .

Forms
• **Present:**
I/You/We/They   determine
He/She/It   determines
Past: determined

Family
• **Noun:** determination

Word Partners
• help (me/you/us/them) determine
• after studying _____ , (I/we/you/they) determined

Examples
• Checking several online reviews **helped me determine** the best video game to buy for my friend's birthday.
• **After studying** the schedule, **we determined** that the train leaving at 11:30 a.m. would get us to the stadium in time for the 2:00 p.m. game.

✏️ **Try It**
Our teacher asked us to help her **determine** the number of students who had not yet turned in their _____ for the field trip.

VERBAL PRACTICE

Talk about it   Discuss ideas with your partner, listen to classmates, and then write your favorite idea.

Discuss
Listen
Write

1. Before starting a game, my friends use Rock-Paper-Scissors to **determine** who should play _____ .

2. If we wanted to **determine** how much sugar is in a can of soda, we could _____

_____ .

determine
verb

Collaborate

Discuss
Agree
Write
Listen

Discuss ideas with your partner and agree on the best words to complete the frame. ▶

After reviewing the details in the story *The True Story of the Three Little Pigs* by Jon Scieszka we _____ that the wolf was not cruel, he was actually _____ .

Our Turn

Discuss
Listen
Write

Read the prompt. Work with the teacher to complete the frames. Write a thoughtful response that includes a convincing reason. ▶

PROMPT: What can you do to determine whether you should go along with the group?

To _____ whether to go along with a group's decision, you should first consider if it is a good or bad _____ . If you focus on the consequences, you might _____ that your action could have a negative result.

Be an Academic Author

Write
Discuss
Listen

Read the prompt and complete the frames. Strengthen your response with a convincing reason. ▶

PROMPT: If someone tells you something about your favorite singer that you think might be false, what would be one way to determine whether the statement is true?

One way to _____ whether a statement is true is to find out news about the singer (in/on) _____ the _____ . It is also important to make sure that the news source is _____ because it will help you conclude what is really true.

Construct a Response

Write
Discuss
Listen

Read the prompt and construct a thoughtful response. Include a relevant example to strengthen your response. ▶

PROMPT: If you received a special invitation from the mayor of your town to attend a ceremony and accept an outstanding student award, how would you determine what to wear to the event?

_____

_____

_____

_____

grammar tip ▶

An **adjective** describes, or tells about, a noun. An adjective sometimes appears after verbs such as *is, was, smell, smelled, taste,* and *tasted.*

EXAMPLE: The grocer knew that the mango was **unripe** because it was **green** and tasted **sour.**

communicate
verb

com • **mu** • ni • cate

 Write it: _____   **Write it again:** _____

 _____

Meaning
to share ideas by talking or writing or in another way

Synonyms
- discuss; share; give information

Examples
- Many friends use _____ to **communicate** with each other.

- His little sister was able to **communicate** the secret about the party by _____ in his ear.

Forms
- **Present:**
  I/You/We/They communicate
  He/She/It   communicates
- **Past:** communicated

Family
- **Noun:** communication

Word Partners
- communicate ideas/ information
- communicate_____ clearly

Examples
- The video about bullying helped to **communicate information** during the assembly.
- Since my grandmother's doctor was able to **communicate the directions clearly**, she understood how much medicine to take.

✏️ **Try It**
My dad learned how to fix barbecue _____ because the cooking show chef **communicated** the steps clearly.

VERBAL PRACTICE

Talk about it

Discuss
Listen
Write

Discuss ideas with your partner, listen to classmates, and then write your favorite idea.

1. We enjoy _____ music because it **communicates** exactly how we feel about life and what's important to us.

2. To convince your parents to let you go to a _____ with your friends, it is important to **communicate** your ideas clearly and carefully.

communicate

verb

Collaborate

Discuss
Agree
Write
Listen

Discuss ideas with your partner and agree on the best words to complete the frame. ▶

After we read about J. K. Rowling, we wrote (a/an) _____ _____

speech to _____ the details about her life.

Our Turn

Discuss
Listen
Write

Read the prompt. Work with the teacher to complete the frames. Write a thoughtful response that includes a convincing reason. ▶
PROMPT: What do you think is the best way to communicate with your friends?

I think that the best way to _____ with my friends

is by _____ . One reason I prefer to communicate

this way is because it's easier than sending a letter, and my friends can get my

_____ and _____ immediately.

Be an Academic Author

Write
Discuss
Listen

Read the prompt and complete the frames. Strengthen your response with a relevant example. ▶
PROMPT: When collaborating with others, what are some ways to communicate your ideas clearly?

When collaborating with others, it is important to _____

your ideas clearly. To communicate clearly, it is important to make eye contact, speak

slowly, and use precise _____ .

Construct a Response

Write
Discuss
Listen

Read the prompt and construct a thoughtful response. Include a relevant example to strengthen your response. ▶
PROMPT: People use words and gestures to communicate. Animals also communicate. What are specific ways pets communicate their needs and desires to their owners?

_____

_____

_____

_____

grammar tip ▶

The preposition *to* needs to be followed by a verb in the base form.

EXAMPLE: When my friend called, I tried *to explain* my idea about the party.

conclude

REVIEW: difference *noun*

DAY 1

An important _____ between watching a game live on TV

at home and watching it at the stadium is that the stadium is filled with people who

_____ .

conclude *verb*

DAY 2

After watching *American Idol*, I _____ that the

runner-up (was/was not) _____ extremely

_____ .

DAY 3

Since many of my classmates love to play _____ ,

I can _____ that children like to use

their imagination to build fantasy worlds.

DAY 4

When I compared all pictures in my photo album with the snapshots my aunt took

with her new _____ , I _____

that most pictures taken from a distance looked better than those taken up close.

DAY 5

After the writer completed her research about living (in/on) _____

_____ , she _____ that the

best story to write would be an action adventure.

TOTAL

136

SMART START

REVIEW: conclusion   *noun*

If I saw a fire truck with a ladder leading into a tree, I would _____

that a _____ was stuck up

the tree.

☐

☐

DAY 2

assume   *verb*

Because I saw my neighbor at the animal shelter, I _____

that she was interested in adopting (a/an) _____ _____ .

☐

☐

DAY 3

When my dad did not return my mother's _____ ,

she _____

that he was away from his cell phone or its battery was dead.

☐

☐

DAY 4

You can't _____ that there will not be a test on Friday

even if your teacher is _____ on Thursday.

☐

☐

DAY 5

If your library book is _____ ,

you can _____ that you will have to pay a fine.

☐

☐

TOTAL

137

conclusion

REVIEW: assume *verb*

DAY 1

When I saw the dark clouds and the wind began to blow, I _____

that the storm would last all _____ .

☐
☐

conclusion *noun*

DAY 2

After waiting 20 minutes for my friends, I came to the _____

that they decided to go to the _____

instead.

☐
☐

DAY 3

I could not find my jacket in my backpack when I got home from school, so I came to the

_____ that I had left it

_____ .

☐
☐

DAY 4

During our afternoon walk, my dog refused to go any further, and started panting, so

I came to the _____ that she was

_____ .

☐
☐

DAY 5

Based on the time it took me to run one lap around the track, I drew the _____

that I could run _____

laps in an hour.

☐
☐

TOTAL

⚑ SMART START

DAY 1

REVIEW: conclude   *verb*

When it rained all night, I reached the _____

that I would need to take (a/an) _____

to school the next day.

☐
☐

DAY 2

assumption   *noun*

You can't make an _____ that you and your

_____

will have the same memories after attending the same event.

☐
☐

DAY 3

Some parents make the false _____ that all video games

are _____ .

☐
☐

DAY 4

When the principal came to our classroom immediately after the assembly, I made the

_____ that he was there to

_____ about our behavior.

☐
☐

DAY 5

Based on the exciting ads for the _____ concert

coming to our area, I made the _____

that all my friends would want to attend.

☐
☐

TOTAL

determine

REVIEW: assumption *noun*

DAY 1

When I walked into the kitchen, my _____

came running behind me, and I noticed that her bowl was empty. So I made the

_____ that my brother had forgotten to feed her.

☐
☐

---

determine *verb*

DAY 2

My mother's story about the steps that led to her career helped me _____

how I can become a _____ , too.

☐
☐

DAY 3

My brother's complaints about his sore feet helped me _____

that the safest shoes to wear hiking would be _____ .

☐
☐

DAY 4

You can _____ what the most popular color in class

is by making a list of everyone's favorite color and _____

the color that occurs most often on the list.

☐
☐

DAY 5

To _____ how to

locate the stadium, I studied both paper and _____ maps.

☐
☐

TOTAL

140

**SMART**START

DAY 1

REVIEW: **determine** *verb*

To _____ how many socks are on the feet of your classmates, you can count the number of _____ and multiply by 2.

☐
☐

DAY 2

communicate *verb*

When a police officer directs traffic, she uses her hands to _____ her _____ .

☐
☐

DAY 3

The fast food restaurant used a billboard along the highway to _____ information about its new _____ .

☐
☐

DAY 4

When the _____ sends a note home to your parent/guardian, it is generally to _____ something important.

☐
☐

DAY 5

The weather map clearly _____ details about the sunny weather we can expect for the next two _____ .

☐
☐

TOTAL

Argument

To make an **argument** means to explain why you believe something is true by supporting it with convincing reasons, relevant examples, and personal experiences.

 Find It Read the sentences. Underline the best reason, example, or experience to support each argument.

1. Young children should get plenty of rest.

   a. Research shows that 8 hours of sleep helps kids stay healthy.
   b. One reason is that cold winters make many people sleepy.
   c. For example, some children enjoy staying up late playing video games.

2. Eating too much sugar is unhealthy.

   a. One reason is that many children enjoy drinking sodas.
   b. For example, school lunches have too many sweets and desserts.
   c. In my experience, I have friends who have cavities from eating too much candy.

 Try It Write one convincing reason to support the argument.

Schools should provide at least 15 minutes for recess. One important reason is that

students _____ .

RATE WORD KNOWLEDGE

Rate how well you know Toolkit words you'll use when you prepare to argue.

3rd Grade	BEFORE	RATE IT — 4th Grade	AFTER	5th Grade
discussion	1 2 3 4	**opinion**	1 2 3 4	perspective
believe	1 2 3 4	**fact**	1 2 3 4	persuade
reason	1 2 3 4	**argument**	1 2 3 4	position
agree	1 2 3 4	**convince**	1 2 3 4	reasonable
disagree	1 2 3 4	**evidence**	1 2 3 4	support
experience	1 2 3 4	**convincing**	1 2 3 4	opposing

DISCUSSION GUIDE

- Form groups of four.
- Assign letters to each person.
- Each group member takes a turn leading a discussion.
- Prepare to report about one word.

Ⓐ Ⓑ
Ⓓ Ⓒ

DISCUSS WORDS

Discuss how well you know the fourth grade words. Then, report to the class how you rated each word.

GROUP LEADER **Ask**

So, _____ what do you know
(NAME)

about the word _____ ?

GROUP MEMBERS **Discuss**

1 = I **don't recognize** the word _____ .

I need to learn what it means.

2 = I **recognize** the word _____ ,

but I need to learn the meaning.

3 = I'm **familiar** with the word _____ .

I think it means _____ .

4 = I **know** the word _____ .

It's a _____ , and it means _____ .
(PART OF SPEECH)

Here is my example sentence: _____ .

REPORTER **Report Word Knowledge**

Our group gave the word _____ a rating of _____ because _____ .

SET A GOAL AND REFLECT

First, set a vocabulary goal for this unit by selecting at least three words that you plan to thoroughly learn.
At the end of the unit, return to this page and write a reflection about one word you have mastered.

GOAL

During this unit I plan to thoroughly learn the words _____ ,

_____ , and _____ . Increasing my word knowledge will

help me speak and write effectively when I need to argue a point.

As a result of this unit, I feel most confident about the word _____ .

This is my model sentence: _____

_____ .

REFLECTION

opinion

noun

Say it: o • pin • ion

Write it: _____   **Write it again:** _____

_____

TOOLKIT

Meaning
a way of thinking about something

Synonyms
• idea; belief

Antonyms
• fact

Examples
• In the girl's **opinion**, apples are the best fruit because they are sweet and _____ .

• In the doctor's **opinion**, the boy's broken _____ has healed well.

Forms
• **Singular:** opinion
• **Plural:** opinions

Family
• **Adjective:** opinionated

Word Partners
• In (my, your, his/her, our, their) opinion
• strong opinion(s)

Examples
• In **your opinion**, are board games more enjoyable than video games?

• My best friend has a **strong opinion** about sports. She thinks they build teamwork.

Try It

In my **opinion**, it is important to be _____ to a close friend.

VERBAL PRACTICE

Talk about it

Discuss ideas with your partner, listen to classmates, and then write your favorite idea.

Discuss
Listen
Write

1. In my **opinion**, all classrooms should have _____

_____ .

2. My teacher has a strong **opinion** about _____

_____ .

opinion
noun

WRITING PRACTICE

Collaborate

Discuss
Agree
Write
Listen

Discuss ideas with your partner and agree on the best words to complete the frame. ▶

In our _____ , the best day of the week is

_____ because we get to _____ .

Our Turn

Discuss
Listen
Write

Read the prompt. Work with the teacher to complete the frames. Write a thoughtful response that includes a convincing reason. ▶

PROMPT: Do you have a strong **opinion** about what you do at your birthday party?

I have a strong _____ about being able to _____

at my birthday party. One reason I want to do this is because it would be _____

_____ .

Be an Academic Author

Write
Discuss
Listen

Read the prompt and complete the frames. Strengthen your response with a convincing reason. ▶

PROMPT: Do you have an **opinion** about doing homework on the weekend?

In my _____ , doing homework on the weekend is

_____ . I believe this because on the weekend, it is important to

_____ .

Construct a Response

Write
Discuss
Listen

Read the prompt and construct a thoughtful response. Include a convincing reason to strengthen your response. ▶

PROMPT: In your **opinion**, when should children be allowed to watch TV on a school night?

_____

_____

_____

_____

grammar tip ▶

The preposition *to* needs to be followed by a base verb.

EXAMPLE: I believe children should be allowed *to wear* costumes to school on Halloween.

fact
noun

 Write it: _____ **Write it again:** _____

 _____

Meaning	Examples
information that is true	• It is a **fact** that _____ is an important sport in many countries.

Synonyms	• One important **fact** about Dr. Martin Luther King, Jr. is that he _____ for the rights of African Americans.
• information; truth	
Antonyms	
• opinion	

Forms
- **Singular:** fact
- **Plural:** facts

Family
- **Adjective:** factual
- **Adverb:** factually

Word Partners
- important fact

- in fact

Examples
- Two **important facts** to know before school starts is the name of your teacher and the location of your classroom.
- My class is culturally diverse. **In fact**, most students speak two languages.

 **Try It**

An **important fact** to include in an invitation to a birthday party is the _____ .

VERBAL PRACTICE

Talk about it   Discuss ideas with your partner, listen to classmates, and then write your favorite idea.

Discuss
Listen
Write

1. An interesting **fact** about a chameleon is that it can _____ .

2. Two important **facts** that you should include when you write a report about

   an Olympic athlete are the person's _____ and

   _____ .

fact
noun

WRITING PRACTICE

Collaborate

Discuss
Agree
Write
Listen

Discuss ideas with your partner and agree on the best words to complete the frame. ▶

In our opinion, the best way to learn the lyrics of a song is by listening to it

_____ . In _____ ,

we memorized the words to "_____" by

_____ .

Our Turn

Discuss
Listen
Write

Read the prompt. Work with the teacher to complete the frames. Write a thoughtful response that includes a relevant example.

PROMPT: What is one important fact you would tell a new student about your school?

One important _____ about our school is that it has an amazing

_____. In fact, during the school week I always look forward to

_____ .

Be an Academic Author

Write
Discuss
Listen

Read the prompt and complete the frames. Strengthen your response with a convincing reason.

PROMPT: In a report about yourself, what is the most important fact you would include?

The most important _____ I would include in a report about myself is that I am good

at _____. I think this fact is important because it

shows my interest in becoming (a/an) _____ _____ .

Construct a Response

Write
Discuss
Listen

Read the prompt and construct a thoughtful response. Include a relevant example to strengthen your response. ▶

PROMPT: Many adults think that most children do very little around the house. What two facts could you provide to convince an adult that you are helpful and responsible?

_____

_____

grammar tip ▶

An *adverb* describes a verb, an action. Adverbs usually end in *-ly* and come after the verb to describe how the action is done.

EXAMPLE: The athlete ran *quickly* around the track.

argument
noun

 Write it: _____ **Write it again:** _____

 _____

Meaning	Examples
a reason for or against something	• One **argument** for wearing a _____ is that it lowers the risk of injuries in a car accident. 
Synonyms • reasoning; thinking	• The boy's mother made a strong **argument** against buying the new _____ he wanted. 

Forms
- **Singular:** argument
- **Plural:** arguments

Family
- **Verb:** argue

Word Partners
- a strong argument for/ against (something)
- support (my, your, his/her, our, their) argument with (data, evidence, research)

Examples
- My brothers made **a strong argument for** watching the championship game instead of cartoons.
- When I asked my parents to adopt a puppy, I **supported my argument** with many examples of my responsible behavior.

 Try It

To improve my final draft, my teacher made a strong **argument** for checking my _____
_____ .

VERBAL PRACTICE

Talk about it   Discuss ideas with your partner, listen to classmates, and then write your favorite idea.

Discuss
Listen
Write

1. One good **argument** for reading at least 20 minutes every day is that it helps you to

_____ .

2. A strong **argument** against doing homework late at night is that you might

_____ .

argument
noun

WRITING PRACTICE

Collaborate

Discuss
Agree
Write
Listen

Discuss ideas with your partner and agree on the best words to complete the frame. ▶

We can improve our _____ for a computer lab by showing

evidence that it will help us _____ .

Our Turn

Discuss
Listen
Write

Read the prompt. Work with the teacher to complete the frames. Write a thoughtful response that includes a convincing reason. ▶

PROMPT: Give one strong argument for working collaboratively in school.

One strong _____ for having students work collaboratively is that

it allows them to _____ .

For example, when I work with a partner, we discuss ways to

_____ .

Be an Academic Author

Write
Discuss
Listen

Read the prompt and complete the frames. Strengthen your response with a relevant example. ▶

PROMPT: How could you support an argument for recycling at school?

I could support an _____ for recycling at school by

_____ . For example,

I could research about how much _____ and

_____ is thrown away every day in a school.

Construct a Response

Write
Discuss
Listen

Read the prompt and construct a thoughtful response. Include a convincing reason to strengthen your response. ▶

PROMPT: Do you believe that watching too much television is harmful for preschool children? What is one strong argument against allowing children to watch too much TV?

_____

_____

_____

_____

---

grammar tip ▶

Use a verb + *ing* after the prepositions *by*, *of*, and *for*.

EXAMPLE: The documentary showed reasons *for allowing* children to have cell phones.

convince
verb

Say it: con • vince

 Write it: _____   **Write it again:** _____

 _____

TOOLKIT

Meaning	Examples
to make someone believe or do something	• The boy **convinced** his dad to stop working and watch the _____ on TV. 
Synonyms • prove; encourage **Antonyms** • discourage	• Before guests arrive, the girl's mother will try to **convince** her to clean up her _____ . 

Forms
- **Present:**
  I/You/We/They   convince
- He/She/It   convinces
- **Past:** convinced

Family
- **Adjective:** convincing

Word Partners
- (to) convince (someone) to (do something)
- try to convince

Examples
- My coach **convinced me to** get a haircut.
- After hearing my friend sing, the teacher **tried to convince** her that she should audition for the school play.

 **Try It**

My neighbor **convinced** me to _____ while he was away.

VERBAL PRACTICE

Talk about it

Discuss
Listen
Write

Discuss ideas with your partner, listen to classmates, and then write your favorite idea.

1. One of my friends always tries to **convince** me to lend her my favorite _____ _____ .

2. The substitute teacher tried to **convince** us to _____ .

WRITING PRACTICE

Collaborate

Discuss
Agree
Write
Listen

Discuss ideas with your partner and agree on the best words to complete the frame. ▶

In an argument, each person tries to _____ the other

that he or she is right by _____ .

Our Turn

Discuss
Listen
Write

Read the prompt. Work with the teacher to complete the frames. Write a thoughtful response that includes a relevant example. ▶

PROMPT: It is hard to convince some people to try a new food. How difficult or easy is it for your friends to convince you to eat something new or unusual?

It is somewhat (difficult/easy) _____ for my friends to _____

me to eat something new. For example, I recently was offered _____

_____ and (tried/didn't try)

_____ it because it looked _____ .

Be an Academic Author

Write
Discuss
Listen

Read the prompt and complete the frames. Strengthen your response with a convincing reason. ▶

PROMPT: Have you ever seen a commercial that tried to convince you to buy something unhealthy?

Recently, I saw a commercial that tried to _____ me to buy

_____ . In my opinion, this product is unhealthy because it contains

_____ and _____ .

Construct a Response

Write
Discuss
Listen

Read the prompt and construct a thoughtful response. Include a convincing reason to strengthen your response. ▶

PROMPT: Think about a time that a friend convinced you to do something challenging. Explain how this experience helped you try something new and feel proud.

_____

_____

_____

_____

grammar tip ▶

The preposition *to* needs to be followed by a base verb.

EXAMPLE: I tried *to finish* all my homework before dinner.

evidence
noun

Say it: ev • i • dence

 Write it: _____   **Write it again:** _____

 _____

TOOLKIT

Meaning	Examples
facts or information that prove something is true	• There is a lot of **evidence** that eating too much sugar leads to _____ . 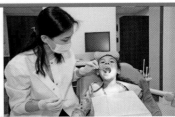
Synonyms • proof; facts	• One piece of **evidence** that the bicycle was in an accident was the seriously bent _____ . 

Forms
• **Singular:** evidence
• **Plural:** evidence

Word Partners
• convincing evidence

• one piece of evidence

Examples
• My friend's perfect score on the spelling test was **convincing evidence** that she had studied every night.
• The smashed window is just **one piece of evidence** that the storm was powerful.

 Try It

The broken plate and frosting all over the floor were **convincing evidence** that my dog had eaten the _____ .

VERBAL PRACTICE

Talk about it

Discuss
Listen
Write

Discuss ideas with your partner, listen to classmates, and then write your favorite idea.

1. The researchers collected **evidence** to show that the water was

_____ .

2. Constant yawning is convincing **evidence** that you are extremely

_____ .

WRITING PRACTICE

Collaborate

Discuss
Agree
Write
Listen

Discuss ideas with your partner and agree on the best words to complete the frame. ▶

To convince our teacher to allow us to _____ during

tests, we need strong _____ that it will help us relax and focus.

Our Turn

Discuss
Listen
Write

Read the prompt. Work with the teacher to complete the frames. Write a thoughtful response that includes a convincing reason. ▶

PROMPT: What is one thing you would change about your neighborhood? What is one piece of evidence you can use to show the change is needed?

One thing I would do to improve my neighborhood is to add more _____ .

One piece of _____ that would convince leaders to make this

addition is that it would help people _____ .

Be an Academic Author

Write
Discuss
Listen

Read the prompt and complete the frames. Strengthen your response with a convincing reason. ▶

PROMPT: If you were selecting a student to lead a class project, what would you consider to be the most important skill? What convincing evidence would help you make your decision?

When selecting a student to lead a class project, one important skill is being able to

_____ . Observing that student

_____ would be convincing

_____ to support my decision.

Construct a Response

Write
Discuss
Listen

Read the prompt and construct a thoughtful response. Include a convincing reason to strengthen your response. ▶

PROMPT: Do you believe that school lunches should include more healthy choices? What convincing evidence supports the argument that school lunch menus need to include more healthy foods?

_____

_____

_____

grammar tip ▶

Noncount nouns name things that can't be counted. Noncount nouns have the same form for "one" or "more than one." Do not add an *-s* to a noncount noun to make it plural.

EXAMPLE: When I get home from a trip, I have to unpack my *luggage* and make sure all of my *homework* is finished.

convincing

adjective

Say it: con • vinc • ing

 Write it: _____ **Write it again:** _____

 _____

TOOLKIT

Meaning
believable

Synonyms
- strong; believable

Antonyms
- weak; unbelievable

Examples
- The dentist's reasons for flossing your _____ were very **convincing**.

- The girl scout was very **convincing,** so my grandmother ordered several boxes of _____ .

Family
- **Verb:** convince

Word Partners
- very convincing
- a convincing reason

Examples
- My older brother's arguments for getting a job were **very convincing**.
- She didn't give her coach **a convincing reason** for being late to practice, so she had to run laps.

 Try It

My teacher's letter to parents was **very convincing**, so they volunteered to help with the _____ _____ .

VERBAL PRACTICE

Talk about it

Discuss
Listen
Write

Discuss ideas with your partner, listen to classmates, and then write your favorite idea.

1. Our babysitter gave a **convincing** argument for turning off the TV and _____

_____ .

2. A **convincing** reason to turn off cell phones during _____ is

that they are distracting and annoying.

convincing
adjective

WRITING PRACTICE

Collaborate

Discuss
Agree
Write
Listen

Discuss ideas with your partner and agree on the best words to complete the frame. ▶

One _____ reason to join after school clubs might be to

_____ .

Our Turn

Discuss
Listen
Write

Read the prompt. Work with the teacher to complete the frames. Write a thoughtful response that includes a convincing reason. ▶

PROMPT: Many teachers want their students to improve certain skills. What is one convincing reason that a teacher might use to encourage a class to study or practice that skill daily?

My teacher wants all students in our class to better understand _____

_____ . One _____

reason we need to study or practice daily is that assignments and tests include difficult

_____ .

Be an Academic Author

Write
Discuss
Listen

Read the prompt and complete the frames. Strengthen your response with a relevant example.

PROMPT: What would you consider a very convincing reason for turning in a report late?

A very _____ reason for turning in a report late

might be that you had a _____ problem. For

example, once I wasn't able to turn in an important assignment on time because I

_____ , and my teacher was understanding.

Construct a Response

Write
Discuss
Listen

Read the prompt and construct a thoughtful response. Include a convincing reason to strengthen your response. ▶

PROMPT: There are many reasons to wear protective gear such as a helmet when you play a sport. What do you consider the most convincing reason for protective gear?

_____

_____

_____

grammar tip ▶

Count nouns name things that can be counted. Count nouns have two forms, singular and plural. To make most count nouns plural, add **-s**. To make count nouns that end in *x, ch, sh, ss,* and *z,* plural, add **-es**.

EXAMPLE: In autumn, the *leaves* fall from the *trees*.

opinion

SMART *START*

DAY 1

REVIEW: **communicate**   *verb*

I usually _____ with my

friends by _____ them.

DAY 2

opinion   *noun*

In my _____ ,

the best singer is _____ .

DAY 3

My (mother/father/aunt) _____ has strong _____

about _____ .

DAY 4

Sometimes it's hard to keep other people's _____ from

influencing the way I _____ .

DAY 5

In my _____ , you have to work hard in

order to _____ .

TOTAL

156

SMART START

REVIEW: opinion   *noun*

DAY 1

In my _____ , our

student council president should be elected by all the students based on his or her

_____ .

☐

☐

fact   *noun*

DAY 2

It was very hot yesterday. In _____ , the

heat was the reason we decided to _____

in the afternoon.

☐

☐

DAY 3

We were told to include only the most important _____

in our reports about the terrible _____

we saw.

☐

☐

DAY 4

Before we decide what to do about the problem of _____

in our community, we need to look at the _____ .

☐

☐

DAY 5

I thought the game was this Friday. In _____ ,

it isn't until next _____ .

☐

☐

TOTAL

argument

SMART START

REVIEW: fact *noun*

DAY 1

You should include important _____
to support your ideas in every _____
you prepare.

argument *noun*

DAY 2

A strong _____
for daily exercise is that you will _____
_____.

DAY 3

I can support my _____
that sleep is important with _____
from scientific reports.

DAY 4

There are many strong _____ for protecting the
environment, such as our need for _____
_____.

DAY 5

What _____ did the teacher make
for not allowing students to _____
_____?

TOTAL

SMART START

REVIEW: argument *noun*

DAY 1

According to my parents, I rarely have a good _____ for

_____

later than they think I should.

convince *verb*

DAY 2

I tried to _____ my father to

_____ , but he wouldn't.

DAY 3

My friend did not want to _____ with me, but I was

finally able to _____

(him/her) _____ .

DAY 4

The purpose of a TV commercial is to _____ people to

_____ something.

DAY 5

You will have a very hard time trying to _____ me to

_____ the party.

TOTAL

evidence

SMARTSTART

REVIEW: convince *verb*

DAY 1

I would like to _____ my parents

to let me _____

_____ .

---

evidence *noun*

DAY 2

After reviewing the _____ he found in the cafeteria, the janitor

concluded that several _____

had a food fight during lunch.

DAY 3

The photos of the girl's injuries present convincing _____

that skateboarding can be _____

_____ .

DAY 4

The school principal accused the student of _____ ,

but he could not provide one piece of _____

to support his claim.

DAY 5

The fact that you're becoming stronger, faster, and more flexible is all convincing

_____ that your exercise plan

is _____ .

TOTAL

 **SMART START**

REVIEW: evidence *noun*

DAY 1

The paw prints and unpleasant odor provided strong _____

that a _____ had entered the apartment.

☐
☐

---

convincing *adjective*

DAY 2

His excuse for not having his _____

finished was not very _____ .

☐
☐

DAY 3

One _____ reason for you to keep your bedroom

clean is that you can _____

_____ .

☐
☐

DAY 4

In my report, I gave some _____

arguments for _____

the environment.

☐
☐

DAY 5

The students did not have a _____

explanation for being so _____ during their

classmate's presentation.

☐
☐

TOTAL

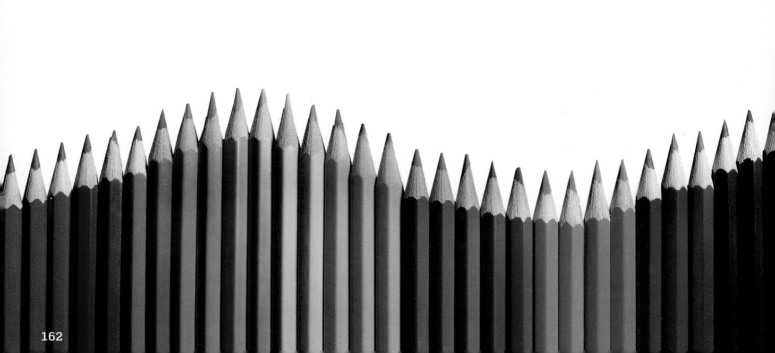

▶ grammar lessons

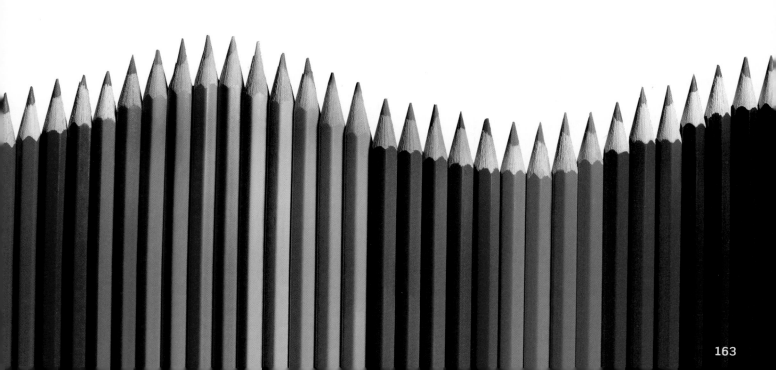

grammar

▶ **Present Tense Verbs**

Use the **present tense** when you talk about actions that happen usually, sometimes, or regularly.

	Subject	Verb
Use the **base form** of the verb when the subject is *I, you, we,* or *they*.	I You We They	**record** the music. base form
Use the **-s** form of the verb when the subject is *he, she,* or *it*.	He She It	**record**s the music. -s form

- When the base form of the verb ends in **s, sh, ch,** or **x,** add **-es:**
  miss ➝ *misses;* *wash* ➝ *washes;* *catch* ➝ *catches;* *fix* ➝ *fixes*
- When the base form of the verb ends in a consonant + **y,** change the **y** to **i** and add **-es:** *cry* ➝ *cries*

🔍 Find It

Read the sentences. Write the correct form of the present tense verb.

1. Levi (eat/eats) _____ cereal for breakfast.

2. We (play/plays) _____ outside after school.

3. My friends (want/wants) _____ a snack during recess.

4. The plant (need/needs) _____ water and sunlight.

✏️ Try It

Complete the sentences using the correct form of the verb.

1. Jenna (read) _____ a new book every week.

2. My cousin (watch) _____ too much television.

3. Anton and Matt (think) _____ math is interesting.

4. My friend and I (ride) _____ our bikes to the park on Saturdays.

Discuss and Write

Collaborate

Discuss
Agree
Write
Listen

Work with a partner. Use the correct form of the present tense verbs to complete the sentences.

1. brush/
read

Matt _____ his teeth, and then
_____ before bed every night.

2. call/arrive

My friend usually _____ her parents as soon
as she _____ home from school.

3. bark/jump

The dog _____ when she is sad and
_____ when she is excited .

Your Turn

Think
Write

Work independently. Use the correct form of the present tense verbs and your own words to complete the sentences.

1. try/play

Every day after school, Vanessa _____
to practice the violin before she _____ video
games with her _____ .

2. agree/
promise

Sofia _____ that skateboarding can be
_____ , so she _____
to be careful and always wear a helmet.

3. need/want

Maya and Armando _____ to ask their teacher
for permission if they _____ to go to the
_____ .

4. complete/
meet

After school on Fridays, we always _____
our homework early because we like to _____
our friends at the _____ on Saturday.

grammar

▶ **Adjectives and Adverbs**

An **adjective** describes a noun.
An **adverb** describes a verb.

Adjective	Adverb
She sang a **beautiful** song.	She sang **beautifully.**
I have a **loud** family.	My brother speaks **loudly.**
My older sister is a **careful** driver.	She drives **carefully.**

- An adjective usually comes before the noun it describes. An adjective can also come directly after the verb *be*: New York City is big.
- An adverb usually comes after the verb it describes. Most adverbs are formed by adding *-ly* to an adjective: careful → carefully

🔍 Find It

Complete the sentences with either the adjective or the adverb.

1. On the first day of school there are always many (nervous/nervously)

_____ students.

2. She speaks so (quick/quickly) _____ that it's sometimes difficult to

understand her.

3. Mary is an (honest/honestly) _____ person who would never lie.

4. The car skidded (wild/wildly) _____ and almost crashed.

✏️ Try It

Complete the sentences using the correct form (adjective or adverb) of the word.

1. I was a (shy) _____ child a few years ago, but now I am much

more outgoing.

2. Can you please speak more (slow) _____?

3. Gorillas are (intelligent) _____ animals.

4. My teacher always reminds us to write (neat) _____ .

Discuss and Write

Collaborate

Discuss
Agree
Write
Listen

Work with a partner. Write the sentence, including the adverb or adjective provided.

1. (difficult)   There were some questions on the test.

_____

_____ .

2. (talented)   She is a musician who has won many awards for her music.

_____

_____ .

3. (loudly)   They screamed when they learned that they won the contest.

_____

_____ .

Your Turn

Think
Write

Work independently. Use the correct form (adjective or adverb) of the word and your own words to complete the sentences.

1. (delicious)   Her grandparents cook the most _____

_____ .

2. (nervous)   He spoke _____ when he told his parents that he

broke the _____ .

3. (beautiful)   My mother knits _____

_____ .

4. (soft)   The nurse spoke _____ to the

_____ child.

grammar

▶ Adverbs of Frequency

Use **adverbs of frequency** to talk about how often actions happen.

	Adverbs of Frequency	Examples with the Verb *Be*	Examples with Other Verbs
100%	always	I **am always** home for dinner.	I **always eat** dinner with my family
	usually	She **is usually** cheerful.	She **usually has** a smile on her face.
	often	We **are often** busy during the weekend.	We **often visit** friends on the weekend.
	sometimes	They **are sometimes** bored.	They **sometimes have** nothing to do.
	rarely	My brother **is rarely** tired.	My brother **rarely feels** tired.
0%	never	Emily **is never** late for school.	Emily **never comes** to school late.

- Put adverbs of frequency after the verb *be*.
- Put adverbs of frequency before all other verbs.

Find It

Read the pairs of sentences. Underline the sentence that has the adverb of frequency in the right place.

1. My parents rarely go to bed before 12:00. | My parents go to bed rarely before 12:00.

2. My best friend plays always soccer on Saturday. | My best friend always plays soccer on Saturday.

3. He never is late for school. | He is never late for school.

4. The mail usually comes early in the afternoon. | The mail comes usually early in the afternoon.

Try It

Write the sentences and include the adverb of frequency.

1. (sometimes) She walks home after school.

_____

2. (usually) I speak Spanish with my father.

_____

3. (always) My baby brother is hungry in the morning.

_____

Discuss and Write

Collaborate

Discuss
Agree
Write
Listen

Work with a partner. Complete the sentences using appropriate adverbs of frequency and your own words.

1. We _____ eat _____ because we prefer to eat foods that are healthy.

2. My teacher _____ begins the lesson until everyone is _____ .

3. My cousins _____ visit us every _____ .

4. For my birthday, my family and I _____ go out to a _____ .

Your Turn

Think
Write

Work independently. Complete the sentences using appropriate adverbs of frequency and your own words.

1. I _____ _____ before I go to bed or it's hard for me to fall asleep.

2. Karen _____ brings _____ to school for lunch.

3. I am _____ happy after spending time with my _____ .

4. My mother _____ gets a sunburn because she is careful to put on _____ when it is sunny out.

grammar

▶ **Present Progressive Tense**

Use the **present progressive** to talk about an action that is happening right now.

Subject	be	Verb + *ing*
I	am	
He She It	is	listen**ing** to a popular band.
You We They	are	

- To form the progressive tense of most verbs, add **-ing** to the base form of the verb: read ⟶ *reading*
- For verbs that end in a consonant + **-e**, drop the –e before adding *-ing*: dance ⟶ *dancing*

🔍 Find It

Complete the sentences using the correct form of the verb.

1. We're (wait) _____ for the rain to stop so we can go outside.

2. My mother is (plant) _____ flowers in the garden.

3. I am (do) _____ my homework now so that I can go out later.

4. Mario's family is (visit) _____ his grandmother in Florida.

✏️ Try It

Read the present tense sentences. Write the sentences as present progressive sentences.

1. The dog chases its own tail.

   _____

2. Ethan and Lucy wave to each other from across the street.

   _____

3. The basketball player dribbles the ball across the court.

   _____

grammar
▶ **Present Progressive Tense**

Discuss and Write

Collaborate

Discuss
Agree
Write
Listen

Work with a partner. Use the correct form of the verbs to complete the sentences.

1. sleep/snore

My uncle is _____ in the living room armchair

and _____ loudly!

2. pull/push

My little brother is _____ the wagon of toys

from the front, and his friend is _____ it from

the back.

3. bang/stomp

She is _____ the drum and

_____ her feet to the music.

Your Turn

Think
Write

Work independently. Use the correct form of the verb and your own words to complete the sentences.

1. look

John is _____ under the couch for his

_____ .

2. cry

The little girl is _____ because she dropped

her _____ .

3. snow

Let's go out and make _____

while it's still _____ .

4. throw

The girl is _____ a

_____ for the dog to chase.

grammar
▶ **Past Tense Verbs**

Use the **past tense** to talk about events or actions that have already happened.

Subject	Base Form of Verb + -ed/-d	
I He She It You We They	work**ed**	on the project last night.

- To form the simple past tense of most regular verbs, add **-ed** to the base form of the verb: *listen* ⟶ **listened**
- For regular verbs that end in **-e**, add **-d**: *smile* ⟶ **smiled**

Find It

Read the sentences. Complete the sentences using the correct form of the verb.

1. Maria (lives/lived) _____ in California until she was 5 years old.

2. The dog (barks/barked) _____ at the new mail carrier whenever the

mail carrier comes near our house.

3. I (listen/listened) _____ to music after dinner every night.

4. It (rains/rained) _____ the weekend of our camping trip.

Try It

Complete the sentences using the correct form of the verb.

1. My older sister (help) _____ me with a difficult math problem last night.

2. My friends and I (dress) _____ like ghosts last Halloween.

3. I (learn) _____ to ride a bike when I was in kindergarten.

4. John (erase) _____ the writing on the board before Ella had a chance

to copy it.

grammar
▶ **Past Tense Verbs**

Discuss and Write

Collaborate

Discuss
Agree
Write
Listen

Work with a partner. Use the correct form of the verbs to complete the sentences.

1. open/
close

We _____ the window when it got too warm,

and _____ it when it got too cold.

2. cough/
sneeze

I _____ and

_____ a lot when I first got this cold.

3. order/wait

The customers _____ food and then

_____ nearly an hour before it was served.

Your Turn

Think
Write

Work independently. Use the correct form of the verbs and your own words to complete the sentences.

1. call/want

My friend _____ to ask

if I _____ to go to the

_____ with her.

2. smile/
laugh

The audience _____ while they watched the

clown and _____ out loud when he squirted

water at the _____ .

3. dance/play

My friend _____ in our school talent

show last week and I _____ the

_____ .

4. want/ask

I _____ to buy a new

_____ for school so I

_____ my mother if we could go shopping.

grammar

▶ **Possessive Nouns**

Use **possessive nouns** to show that something belongs to someone.

	Singular Noun	Possessive Noun	Example
To show that something belongs to someone, add an apostrophe (') and **-s** to a singular noun.	friend	friend**'s**	My friend**'s** family is large.

	Plural Noun that ends in -s	Possessive Noun	Example
To show that something belongs to more than one person, add an apostrophe (') at the end of a plural noun, following the –s.	friends	friends**'**	My friends' school is in a different neighborhood.

🔍 Find It

Complete the sentences with the correct possessive noun.

1. The (team's/teams') _____ t-shirts are different colors.

2. We go to my (grandparent's/grandparents') _____ house every Friday.

3. I can't get that (movie's/movies') _____ theme song out of my head.

4. A male (lion's/lions's) _____ roar can be heard from as far as five miles away.

✏️ Try It

Complete the sentences with the correct possessive noun.

1. (Emma) _____ report card showed a lot of improvement in math this year.

2. All of the (dolls) _____ clothes had small marks, so the dolls were on sale.

3. Some (frogs) _____ skin can change color to match their environment.

4. Did you know that the (band) _____ drummer is also a singer?

Discuss and Write

Collaborate

Discuss
Agree
Write
Listen

Work with a partner. Read the first sentence. Then complete the second sentence with the correct possessive noun.

1. The names of my sisters are Julie and Karen.

   My _____ names are Julie and Karen.

2. Red and green are the colors of our school.

   Our _____ colors are red and green.

3. The students gave the teacher a framed picture as a gift.

   The _____ gift to the teacher was a framed picture.

4. The glare of the sun made it difficult to see.

   The _____ glare made it difficult to see.

Your Turn

Think
Write

Work independently. Complete the sentences with the correct possessive form of the noun and your own words.

1. (family)   My _____ favorite food is

   _____ , so we eat it all the time!

2. (hamster)   You need to clean your _____

   _____ .

3. (Alex)   _____ foot hurt for days after he dropped a

   _____ on it.

4. (computers) All of the _____ keyboards are

   _____ so I can't use them.

grammar
▶ **There, Their, They're**

There, **their**, and **they're** are homophones. Homophones are words that have the same sound but are spelled differently and have different meanings.

Word	Explanation	Example
there	*There* is an adverb that means *that place*. *There* is also used with the verb *be* to introduce a sentence or clause.	The classroom is over **there**. **There** are 365 days in a year.
their	*Their* shows ownership. It is always followed by a noun.	The children like **their** classroom.
they're	*They're* is a contraction formed by putting together the words *they* + *are*.	**They're** late for class.

🔍 Find It

Read the sentences. Choose the correct word to complete the sentences.

1. My brothers got the flu last week, but (their/they're) _____ starting

   to feel a bit better.

2. The students read (their/they're) _____ essays in front of the class.

3. I lost my jacket but then I found it over (there/their) _____ .

4. (There/Their) _____ are over 300 million people in America!

✏️ Try It

Complete the sentences using there, their, or they're.

1. _____ are so many places I'd like to visit when I'm older.

2. James and Ian are so lucky. _____ mother packs them homemade

   treats for dessert every day.

3. Asia and Africa are very big. In fact, _____ the two largest continents

   in the world.

grammar

Discuss and Write

Collaborate

Discuss
Agree
Write
Listen

Work with a partner. Complete the sentences using *there*, *their*, and *they're*.

1. I recognize _____ faces, but I can't remember

   _____ names.

2. Callie and Rosa are having a party. _____ good friends with

   Sarah so she is helping them plan _____ party.

3. Ben and Julie are coming with me after class. _____ is an

   ice cream shop near my home that sells _____ favorite

   flavor.

Your Turn

Think
Write

Work independently. Complete the sentences with *there*, *their*, and *they're* and your own words.

1. It's hard to believe that _____ weren't any

   _____ 200 years ago.

2. They asked the waiter to take _____ soup back because it

   was too _____ .

3. _____ usually great friends, but sometimes they argue

   about _____ things.

4. I put my _____ down on the table at the back of the room,

   but now it's not _____ .

grammar

▶ **Modal Verbs**

A **modal verb** is a helping verb that adds more meaning to the main verb.

Example Sentences	Subject	Modal	Base Form of Verb		Meaning
The snow **could** fall all through the night.	The snow	**could**	fall	all through the night.	Use *could* to show that something might be possible.
We **should** study for the test.	We	**should**	study	for the test.	Use *should* to make suggestions or recommendations.
She **would** go to Maria's house if she had someone to drive her.	She	**would**	go	to Maria's house if she had someone to drive her.	Use *would* to show that something is possible under certain conditions.

🔍 Find It

Read the sentences. Complete the sentences with the best modal choice.

1. You look exhausted! You (should/would) _____ go to bed early.

2. I (could/should) _____ come to your house after school on Monday,

   Wednesday, or Friday, but I'm not free on Tuesday or Thursday.

3. He (would/should) _____ take a picture if the camera wasn't broken.

✏️ Try It

Complete the sentences with the correct modal + verb forms.

1. Eva's mother said that for her birthday she (could + invite / could + invited)

   _____ four friends for a sleepover.

2. He has a great voice. He (should + enter / should + enters) _____ a

   singing competition.

3. My brother said he (would + wash / would + washed _____ the dishes

   if I dried them.

Discuss and Write

Collaborate

Discuss
Agree
Write
Listen

Work with a partner. Complete the sentences with the best modal choices. Use the modals _could_, _should_, and _would_.

1. Our sisters _____ meet. I think they

_____ like each other.

2. We _____ probably lift heavier boxes, but we

_____ hurt ourselves.

3. We _____ get there anytime between 5:00 and 6:00. What

time do you think we _____ get there?

4. We _____ play ball this afternoon, but we

_____ probably go home and do our homework first.

Your Turn

Think
Write

Work independently. Choose the best modal and your own words to complete the sentences. Use the modals _could, should,_ and _would_.

1. You keep getting cavities. You _____ eat less

_____ .

2. My baby brother _____ break every

_____ in the house if we didn't put them on the top shelves.

3. Our school _____ form a

_____ club. A lot of people would join.

4. I _____ buy lots of _____

if I got a gift certificate for my birthday.

Acknowledgments, continued from page ii

iv (tl) ©Blend Images Alamy, (cr) ©Olesya Feketa/Shutterstock.com, (cr) ©iofoto/Shutterstock.com, (b) ©Lisa F. Young/Shutterstock.com. vi (tl), ©kitty/Shutterstock.com, (cr) ©Digital Media Pro/Shutterstock.com, (cl) ©Betsie Van der Meer/Getty Images, (b) ©Tim Gainey/Alamy. viii (tl) ©iofoto/Shutterstock.com, (cr) ©Mila Supinskaya/Shutterstock.com, (cl) ©Olena Brodetska/Shutterstock.com, (b) ©Bonnie Taylor Barry/Shutterstock.com. x, (tl) ©Tim Dalek/Getty Images, (cr) ©michaeljung/Shutterstock.com, (cl) ©AAraujo/Shutterstock.com, (b) ©Comstock/Getty Images. 2 (tr) ©Blend Images/Alamy. 4 (t) ©Lisa F. Young/Shutterstock.com, (b) ©Dawn Shearer-Simonetti/Shutterstock.com. 6 (t) ©Fuse/Getty Images, (b) ©Andresr/Shutterstock.com. 8 (t) ©Olesya Feketa/Shutterstock.com, (b) ©naluwan/Shutterstok.com. 10 (t) ©Luis Louro/Shutterstock.com, (b) ©Siede Preis/Getty Images. 12 (t) ©Joy Fera/Shutterstock.com, (b) ©greenland/Shutterstock.com. 14 (t) ©Darrin Henry/Shutterstock.com, (b) ©Gerald Marella/Shutterstock.com. 22 (cr) ©Mitsuaki Iwago/Minden Pictures, (b) "Giant Panda" ©National Geographic. 24 (t) ©bikeriderlondon/Shutterstock.com, (b) ©GlowImages/Alamy. 26 (t) ©iofoto/Shutterstock.com, (b) ©Lisa F. Young/Shutterstock.com. 28 (t) ©Rob Marmion/Shutterstock.com, (b) ©Agnieszka Kirinicjanow/E+/Getty Images. 30 (t) ©iStockphoto.com/stevecoleimages, (b) ©kaczor58/Shutterstock.com. 32 (t) ©puwanai/Shutterstock.com, (b) ©David Roth/The Image Bank/Getty Images. 34 (t) ©WilleeCole/Shutterstock.com, (b) ©papkin/Shutterstock.com. 42 (tr) ©kitty/Shutterstock.com. 44 (t) ©David Buffington/Photodisc/Getty Images, (b) ©Blend Images/Shutterstock.com. 46 (t) ©Pavel Ilyukhin/Shutterstock.com, (b) ©Dustie/Shutterstock.com. 48 (t) ©Kristian sekulic/E+/Getty Images, (b) ©Monkey Business Images/Shutterstock.com. 50 (t) ©KidStock/Blend Images/Getty Images, (b) ©Digital Media Pro/Shutterstock.com. 52 (t) ©NigelSpiers/Shutterstock.com, (b) ©Rob Marmion/Shutterstock.com. 54 (t) ©Rich Legg/Vetta/Getty Images, (b) ©Sergiy Bykhunenko/Shutterstock.com. 62 (tr) ©Tim Gainey/Alamy. 64 (t) ©Betsie Van der Meer/Getty Images, (b) ©Ant Clausen/Shutterstock.com. 66 (t) ©bikeriderlondon/Shutterstock.com, (b) ©Tom Gowanlock/Shutterstock.com. 68 (t) ©adisornfoto/Shutterstock.com, (b) ©Sergey Yechikov/Shutterstock.com. 70 (t) ©Aspen Photo/Shutterstock.com, (b) ©wong yu liang/Shutterstock.com. 72 (t) ©ERproductions Ltd/Blend Images/Alamy, (b) ©Goodluz/Shutterstock.com. 74 (t) ©Suzanne Tucker/Shutterstock.com, (b) ©Sergiy Zavgorodny/Shutterstock.com. 82 (tr) ©iofoto/Shutterstock.com. 84 (t) ©eAlisa/Shutterstock.com, (b) ©Yuri Samsonov/Shutterstock.com. 86 (t) ©Galina Barskaya/Shutterstock.com, (b) ©Mila Supinskaya/Shutterstock.com. 88 (t) ©PhotoSky/Shutterstock.com, (b) ©ZouZou/Shutterstock.com. 90 (t) ©Tyler Olson/Shutterstock.com, (b) ©wow/Shutterstock.com. 92 (t) ©Pavel IlyukhinShutterstock.com, (b) ©Denizo71/Shutterstock.com. 94 (t) ©PhotoDisc/Getty Images, (b) ©AlexandreNunes/Shutterstock.com. 102 (inset) Iconotec, (tr) ©Raymond Gregory/Shutterstock.com. 104 (t) ©song_mi/Shutterstock.com, (b) ©Olena Brodetska/Shutterstock.com. 106 (t) ©Bonnie Taylor Barry/Shutterstock.com, (b) ©Darrin Henry/Shutterstock.com. 108 (t) ©diplomedia/Shutterstock.com, (b) ©Tristan3D/Shutterstock.com. 110 (t) ©szefei/Shutterstock.com, (b) ©VILevi/Shutterstock.com. 112 (b) ©cynoclub/Shutterstock.com, (b) ©Tracy Whiteside/Shutterstock.com. 114 (t) ©Manamana/Shutterstock.com, (b) ©VaLiza/Shutterstock.com. 122 (tr) ©Mira/Alamy. 124 (t) ©Steve Cukrov/Alamy, (b) ©Charlotte Erpenbeck/Shutterstock.com. 126 (t) ©Wendy Nero/Shutterstock.com, (b) ©Elena Elisseeva/Shutterstock.com. 128 (t) ©Andi Berger/Shutterstock.com, (b) ©michaeljung/Shutterstock.com. 130 (t) ©Utekhina Anna/Shutterstock.com, (b) ©ApollofotoShutterstock.com. 132 (t) ©Andi Berger/Shutterstock.com, (b) ©iPhone/Alamy. 134 (t) ©Vladimir Mucibabic/Shutterstock.com, (b) ©Alena Ozerova/Shutterstock.com. 142 (tr) ©Comstock/Getty Images. 144 (t) ©Dann Tardiff/LWA/Blend Images/Corbis, (b) ©Wavebreak Media LTD/Wavebreak Media Ltd./Corbis. 146 (t) ©Rnoid/Shutterstock.com, (b) ©James P. Blair/National Geographic Creative. 148 (t) ©Blend Images/Shutterstock.com, (b) ©JNP/Shutterstock.com. 150 (t) ©Jamie Grill/Blend Images/Alamy, (b) ©Monkey Business Images/Shutterstock.com. 152 (t) ©Jacqueline Veissid/Stockbyte/Getty Images, (b) ©Willem Havenaar/Shutterstock.com. 154 (t) ©AAraujo/Shutterstock.com, (b) ©The Washington Post/Getty Images.